CHOOSING A LIFE
OF VICTORY

LIFEWORK PRESS

CHOOSING A LIFE OF VICTORY

Seven Powerful Principles
on How to Walk as a "Son" of God
in the Earth

GLORIA GODSON

LIFEWORK PRESS

CHOOSING A LIFE OF VICTORY
Seven Powerful Principles on How to Walk as a Son of God in the Earth

LifeWork Ministries, Inc.
P. O. Box 56
Townsend, DE 19734
www.lifeworkministries.org
lifeworkministriesinc@gmail.com

LifeWork Press ©

2021 by Gloria Godson

All rights reserved solely by the author. No part of this book may be reproduced in any form without the permission of the author. For permission requests, contact author at lifeworkministriesinc@gmail.com.

Unless otherwise indicated, Scripture quotations taken from the Holy Bible, New Living Translation (NLT). Copyright ©1996, 2004, 2007 by Tyndale House Foundation. Used by permission of Tyndale House Publishers, Inc.
Scripture quotations taken from the King James Version (KJV)–*public domain*.

Printed in the United States of America.

ISBN-978-5-0539-0035-4

Dedicated to
Emmanuel, Timothy, and Rhema
and
My friend and partner Holy Spirit

TABLE OF CONTENTS

Introduction
CHAPTER 1—The New Deal 1
CHAPTER 2—A Portrait of New Covenant Sonship 22
CHAPTER 3—Seven Powerful Principles on How to Walk as a "Son" of God in the Earth.. 41
CHAPTER 4—Jesus, God's Sonship Pattern 92
CHAPTER 5—Manifestations: Stories and Photos of People Who Applied These Principles with Amazing Results 110
   i.   Triumph over Cerebral Palsy (The Story of Matthew).....111
   ii. Miracle Deliverance and Healing
      (The Story of Sanae and Linda) 129
   iii. Death of a Child (The Story of Ron Jr.) 150
   iv. Our Identity in Christ (The Story of Vivalyn) 168
   v.   Broken, Restored, and Hopeful (The Story of Erin).........175
   vi. Emotional Healing—Sexual Abuse and
      Divorce (The Story of Alani) 190
   vii. From Janitor to Corporate Officer (The Story of Ken) 197
Conclusion 210

INTRODUCTION

In 2005, I taught the sonship principles discussed in this book at a prayer conference. Preparing for and teaching that message activated in me a passion to walk the earth as a true "son" of God. I wanted to live a life that counted every day. I wanted to make a difference. I purposed in my heart to make kingdom impact wherever I went so that whatever path I walked in life, there would be evidence to anyone who came behind me in the journey of life that I passed that way. I wanted to see evidence of hearts encouraged, faith strengthened, destinies built, and lives transformed by the love and power of God.

I wanted to have all that Jesus purchased for me on the cross. I wanted the new life and covenant that He secured by His death, burial, and resurrection. I determined to leave nothing on the table. I wanted to bring to Jesus the rewards of His suffering. He died for me to be healed. So, I purposed to walk in divine health. He paid for me to live an abundant life, so I purposed to reject and oppose lack, poverty, and want in all its forms and in every area of my life.

> *Jesus paid the full price for me. I will not give myself away at a discount!*

Jesus died to give me His name, authority, and identity. So, I purposed to oppose and reject every attempt by anything or anyone to limit, defraud, label, diminish, or rob me of my true identity in

Christ. I know who I am and whose I am. Jesus paid the full price for me. I will not give myself away at a discount!

Thus, a commitment to operate as a "son" of God was born in my heart—born out of a passion to be all that I can be and more importantly, to be all that God created me to be. The sonship mandates, principles, and patterns discussed in this book became the guiding principles, guard rails, and convictions of my life. It became a way of life, a pattern of thought, and a process framework for me. I prayed them, taught them, challenged myself and others to live by them, and believed them with all my heart.

In 2006, the devil threw "the kitchen sink" at me. He had a meeting with his demons, and the primary question was "What will we do to Gloria to take her out and completely neutralize her?" They came up with a long brainstorming list of potential options. The devil studied the list for a while and then said, "Let's do it all at once!" In the next few years, he attacked, literally, every area of my life—my marriage, my children, my job, my health and my finances—and I was plunged into a very dark time of despair. But the devil came too late! God had already taught me these principles. Tough and heart wrenching as my situation was, I held unto these principles with every fiber of my being. Sometimes, it looked like they were a lie or were not working. Sometimes, my life looked like a reproach, and the devil mocked me. But I held on, despite the fact that my circumstances yelled at me, "Where is your God?" Today, I am still here but only by the grace of God. I am a trophy of the faithfulness and power of Almighty God to keep His promises. I and my children have not only survived; we have thrived. These principles were absolutely fundamental to my sanity, survival, and victory over all that the enemy unleashed. Thanks be to God who always gives us the victory through Christ! I can say with Paul in Romans 8:3 that "In all these things, we are more than conquerors through Christ."

These principles have changed my life. I am no longer a spectator or passive observer in the game of life, just "hoping" that things turn out good. I am an active and vocal participant, engaged in establishing the plan and purpose of God for my life and for the earth. Jeremiah 29:11 states that God has a plan for my future, and He invites me to join Him to establish this plan. Answering the call to sonship is my affirmative response to God's invitation to partner with Him, to bring His awesome plan and purpose to pass in my life.

The principles of sonship discussed in this book were game changers for me and critical to my survival. It was the ladder that God brought down into the pit of despair and devastation where I was. I climbed up and out of the pit to freedom on its rungs.

Who Should Read This Book?

This book is for men and women who have gone through an experience in life that challenged their identity as sons and daughters of God, and caused them to doubt themselves and to question God's love and faithfulness to His word. If you have experienced life circumstances that have brought you to a place that you never imagined that you would ever be, and you wonder, where is God? this book is for you. If life has thrown you a curve ball, and you are under severe stress, but don't have the luxury of "falling apart" because too many people are depending on you, this book is for you.

Maybe you have always been healthy, exercised diligently and eaten right, and out of the blue, you were hit with a medical condition or devastating diagnosis. Or, you have been a faithful spouse, who believed that your marriage commitment would be for life, but instead, you are blindsided by infidelity, separation or divorce. Or maybe, you have been a hard worker and faithful provider for your family, and due to a sudden down turn at work or family situation, you are in a pit financially, and it looks like there is no way out. Or, you have been a faithful parent who modeled the gospel, and labored to raise your children to love God, but instead, they have chosen to go down a path of destruction and you feel helpless. This book is for you! The seven sonship principles in this book will help you to get up out of the ashes, regain control of your life and move forward with confidence. And the sonship pattern in this book will help you to transact in the currency of Isaiah 61:1-3—exchanging ashes for beauty, the oil of joy for mourning, and the garment of praise, for the spirit of heaviness. Reading this book will help you to win!

New Covenant Sonship is Gender Neutral

New covenant sonship is not about gender, rather, it is recognizing the nature, attributes, and capabilities of God within you until it moves you to act like God in the earth. Romans 8:14 makes clear that new covenant sonship is gender neutral. It states "For all who are led by the Spirit of God, are the sons of God." And Romans 8:17 explains further, "If sons, then heirs, heirs of God and joint heirs with Christ." So, in this book, "son(s)" of God and "sonship", refers to the men and women who have made a commitment to grow into maturity in Christ and have learned to hear and obey the voice of the Holy Spirit.

Proclamation

I am a son/daughter of God. I am an heir of God and a joint heir with Christ. I am seated in heavenly places in Christ Jesus. I have the DNA of God. I am a partaker of His divine nature. I have the mind of Christ. I think like God! Jesus died to give me His name, authority, and identity. So, I determine in my heart to oppose and reject every attempt by anyone to limit, defraud, label, diminish, or rob me of my true identity in Christ. I know who I am and whose I am. Jesus paid full price for me. I will not give myself away at a discount! Amen.

THE NEW DEAL

Anything the devil is trying to do in my life today cannot be done because of what Jesus already did on the cross almost 2000 years ago. I cannot be bound, poor, sick, fail, or be oppressed because Jesus has already healed, saved, delivered, and set me free. I am blessed; I cannot be cursed; I am healed; I cannot be sick; I am free; I cannot be bound; I am rich; I cannot be poor. I cannot be cursed, yoked, or defeated because of what Jesus did for me on the cross. I stand in all the finished works of Christ!

CHAPTER 1
THE NEW DEAL

God, who at various times and in various ways spoke in time past to our fathers by the prophets, has in these last days spoken to us by His Son, whom He has appointed heir of all things, through whom also He made the worlds; who being the brightness of His glory and the express image of His person, and upholding all things by the word of His power, when He had by Himself purged our sins, sat down at the right hand of the Majesty on high, having become so much better than the angels, as He has by inheritance obtained a more excellent name than they. (Hebrews 1:1–4)

The New Deal

The book of Hebrews opens with a grand declaration! Heaven is making an announcement. There has been a shift, a clear signal from God that he has initiated a change in the earth. In time past, the book of Hebrews declares that God administered the earth through the agency of prophets who heard from God, spoke with God, and were His channels of communication with the people. However, in these last days, God has made a strategic pivot. He has dispensed with the multitude of prophets and has elevated, announced, and confirmed one person, one voice, one way—His Son! Jesus is the voice and herald of God for these last days. Why? Because the prophets were a foreshadowing of the Son. But now the Son is here, and there is no longer a need for types and shadows. In today's vernacular, God is basically saying the "game" has changed, and if you want to win, you have to change how you play.

> *God has elevated, announced, and confirmed one person, one voice, one way – His Son!*

The scripture proceeds to outline the reasons why God made the Son the focal point of all future engagements 20 and transactions with heaven. The list is long, and it becomes quickly apparent that the prophets do not qualify. Only the Son qualifies. Nobody else comes even close!

The Son

1. Is appointed heir of all things.
2. Is the one through whom God created the worlds.
3. Is the brightness of God's glory.
4. Is the express image of His (God's) person.
5. Upholds all things by the word of His (God's) power.
6. Purged our sins.
7. Sat down at the right hand of the majesty on high.
8. Is so much better than angels.
9. Obtained a more excellent name than the angels.

Only one person fits this description: Jesus the Son of God!

Simply stated, God has initiated a new mold, a new pattern in the earth, a new covenant. The key to understanding and partaking of this new covenant is relationship with the Son. The scripture proceeds to outline the two key indicators and elements of this transition: (1) "He had by Himself purged our sins," referring to the work of Jesus on the cross; and (2) "He has by inheritance obtained a more excellent name." The cross and the name identify the Son and set Him apart as the inaugurator of the new covenant. Let's find out why.

The Cross

Jesus's death on the cross inaugurated a new covenant. Under the new covenant, Christ, the Son, is our only access to God, and walking as "sons" is our only portal to the supernatural power of God. Going forward, success in the Christian walk is acutely dependent on our understanding of the centrality of the Son and our willingness and readiness to walk as "sons" of God in the earth.

> *Christ, the Son, is our only access to God, and walking as "Sons" is our only portal to the supernatural power of God.*

What Did Jesus Do for Us on the Cross?

1. He delivered us from the law and its requirements and made the grace of God available to us—John 1:17. 22.

2. He purchased our freedom with His blood and forgave our sins—Ephesians 1:7.

3. He gave us victory over sin. Sin no longer has dominion over us. It is no longer our master, and we can say *no* to sin— Romans 6:14.

4. He seated us in heavenly places, far above all principalities, powers, dominions, and authorities— Ephesians 2:6.

5. He made us partakers of God's divine nature—1 Peter 1:4.

6. He obliterated all the handwriting of ordinances, legal accusations, and charges the devil had against us—Colossians 2:14.

7. He disarmed the devil and His principalities and powers, disgraced them publicly, and gave us victory over them—Colossians 2:15.

8. He delivered us from every curse. He took upon Himself the curse and gave us the blessings of Abraham—Galatians 3:13.

9. He set us free from every yoke of bondage—Galatians 5:1; John 8:36.

10. He gave us abundant life, to the full, until it overflows—John 10:10.

11. He became poor so that by His poverty, He could make us rich—2 Corinthians 8:9 23.

12. He healed us by the stripes he received— 1 Peter 2:21–25.

13. He made us heirs of God and joint heirs with Himself—Romans 8:17.

14. He gave us exceeding great and precious promises—1 Peter 1:4.

The Power of the Cross

First Corinthians 1:18 states "For the message of the cross is foolishness to those who are perishing, but to us who are being saved it is the power of God."

There is wonder working power in the cross of Jesus Christ. The message of the cross embodies and showcases the redemptive power of God. It tells of the unstoppable power of Almighty God, and His unconditional love, grace and mercy that took a gross instrument of cruelty, horror and death, and used it as an instrument for transformative, redemptive and life-giving purposes. The message of the cross is a message of hope and the power of the cross is the power to take what looked like the world's greatest defeat, and turn it into the greatest victory the world has ever known.

> *At the cross, God redefined power by displaying strength through weakness.*

Billy Graham explains: "When we look at the cross, we see several things:

First, in the cross we see the clearest evidence of the world's guilt. At the cross of Christ, sin reached its climax. Its most terrible display took place at Calvary. It was never blacker nor more hideous. We see the human heart laid bare and its corruption fully exposed.

Second, in the cross we see the strongest proof of God's hatred of sin. God has stated that the soul that sins shall die (Ezekiel 18:20) and that the wages of sin is death (Romans 6:23).

Third, in the cross we see a glorious exhibition of God's love. We look out upon the world of nature, and in the provisions and plans made for our happiness we discover a revelation of God's love. Yet as wonderful as these things are in revealing divine love, nothing is comparable to the sacrifice of Calvary. 'For God so loved the world that he gave his only begotten Son that whoever believes in Him should not perish but have everlasting life' (John 3:16).

Fourth, in the cross we see the way to victory. All of us have at times been defeated by Satan. We are held in bondage to sin and are controlled by the power of the devil. The cross is the instrument by which God delivers us from the penalty of our sins and from the hand of Satan." (Billy Graham, *The Power of the Cross*)

> *The power of the cross is the power to take what looked like the world's greatest defeat, and turn it into the greatest victory the world has ever known.*

The Cross Redefines Power

The word "power" in 1 Corinthians 1:18, is the Greek word *dunamis*, which is frequently used to portray military might or the ability to conquer. It is used two hundred and ten times in the New Testament to describe strength and conquering ability. Its greatest demonstration was through the cross. At the cross, God redefined power by displaying strength through weakness. The devil thought he had won, but he did not know that the cross, which looked like the ultimate display of utter weakness was the greatest manifestation of the power of God, and the symbol of his greatest and overwhelming defeat. Through the cross, Jesus vanquished the devil, took from him the keys of hell and the grave, and rose up to say: "all power in heaven and on earth has been given to me" (Matthew 28:18).

Throughout the world, the power of the cross has proceeded, in every generation, to accomplish the eternal purposes of God. "In the early days of the Church, the message of the Cross - backed with the power of the Spirit – produced life wherever it found open hearts to receive its eternal truth. It ignited new birth in the hearts of men, broke the yoke of spiritual bondage off of people's lives, brought healing to bodies and minds ravaged by sickness and disease, and delivered people of defiling demonic influences from their previous pagan environment" (Rick Renner, The Cross: Foolishness or the power of God). The message and power of the cross is still doing the same today.

The cross declares to the world that it is never over until God says so. He is the Alpha and Omega, the Beginning and the End. He is the King of the universe. He reigns in power and great glory. He is the King of Kings and the Lord of Lords, and with Him, nothing is impossible. If you are in a situation that looks impossible today, do not despair. If you are in a marriage that looks dead, or in a financial or health situation, where the bankers or doctors have spoken death, I challenge you to believe in the power of the cross, and in the God, who is the resurrection and the life. Cry out to Him and He will move on your behalf with the power of the cross, the same power that raised Jesus Christ from the dead.

What a Savior!

Because of the finished works of Christ on Calvary, I am blessed beyond measure. I have access to all the resources of God because of Jesus's work on the cross for me. I could never qualify for God's blessings, goodness, salvation, favor, or deliverance except by placing my faith in the finished works of Christ. Ephesians 2:8 states, for it is by grace you have been saved through faith, and you can't take credit for this, it is a gift from God.

Ephesians 1:4 proceeds to explain that even before he made the world, God loved us and chose us in Christ to be holy and without fault in His eyes. God decided in advance to adopt us into His own family by bringing us to Himself through Jesus Christ. This is what He wanted to do, and it gave Him great pleasure.

> *The name of Jesus is His signet ring! It entitles us to everything that Jesus has and is.*

The scripture is clear! Before I was born, before I had a chance to do good or bad, God loved me, chose me in Christ, and decided to adopt me into His family. So, I do not deserve or merit God's blessings or goodness based on my works, ability, prayer, fasting, obedience, or service. Faith in the finished works of Christ on the cross is my only access and claim to God's forgiveness for my sins and everything else that God has.

Jesus's work is finished, lavish, total, and eternal. I cannot add to it or improve upon it. I simply receive it by faith with deep gratitude and thanksgiving to God. I stand in all the finished works of Christ. Jesus is a package deal! His work of redemption is complete and comprehensive. It includes my salvation, healing, deliverance, prosperity, wellbeing, and so forth. I cannot qualify for or earn any of these. I can only receive them by faith in the Son.

What this means is that anything the devil is trying to do in my life today cannot be done because of what Jesus already did on the cross 2000 years ago. I cannot be bound, poor, sick, fail, or be oppressed because Jesus has already healed, saved, delivered, and set me free. I am blessed; I cannot be cursed; I am healed; I cannot be sick; I am free; I cannot be bound; I am rich; and I cannot be poor. I cannot be cursed, yoked, or defeated because of what Jesus did for me on the cross. I stand in all the finished works of Christ!

The Name

Jesus gave every believer the power to transact kingdom business in His name and as His representative. The name of Jesus is His signet ring! It entitles us to everything that Jesus has and is. When we use the name of Jesus, we are Christ's representative, presenting *all* that Jesus is! Nothing in heaven, on the earth, beneath the earth, in this world, or in the world to come can stop or stand against the mighty name of Jesus!

> *Jesus's work is finished, complete, lavish, total, and eternal. I cannot add to it or improve upon it. I simply receive it by faith.*

In John 14:13–14 (AMP), Jesus said, "And I will do whatever you ask in My name [as My representative], this I will do, so that the Father may be glorified and celebrated in the Son. If you ask Me anything in My name [as My representative], I will do it."

Again, in John 16:23 (AMP), Jesus said, "In that day you will not [need to] ask Me about anything. I assure you and most solemnly say to you, whatever you ask the Father in My name, as My representative, He will give you."

In these scriptures, Jesus, in effect, gave us a power of attorney. A power of attorney is a document that allows you to appoint another person or organization to manage your affairs in your absence or other circumstance. It confers on the recipient the authority to act for another person in all or specified legal or financial matters. A power of attorney can be general or specific. A general power of attorney gives broad powers to the person you appoint as your representative (known as an agent or attorney in fact) to act in your behalf on all matters. A special power of attorney on the other hand, specifies exactly what powers an agent may exercise. For example, you can give a debt collecting agency the authority to collect a specific debt on your behalf. In this example, the debt collection agency's authority to act on your behalf is limited to the specific area that you identified. Jesus gave us a general power of attorney to act on His behalf on all matters in the earth, using His name.

Jesus's name is higher than any other name. Philippians 2:5–11 states:

> Let this mind be in you which was also in Christ Jesus, who, being in the form of God, did not consider it robbery to be equal with God, but made Himself of no reputation, taking the form of a bondservant, and coming in the likeness of men. And being found in appearance as a man, He humbled Himself and became obedient to the point of death, even the death of the cross. Therefore, God also has highly exalted Him and given Him the name which is above every name, that at the name of Jesus every knee should bow, of those in heaven, and of those on earth, and of those under the earth, and that every tongue should confess that Jesus Christ is Lord, to the glory of God the Father.

Jesus voluntarily humbled Himself and took on human flesh; and as a man, He went even further and chose to die an indescribably horrendous death to pay for our salvation. Because of this, He is highly exalted and has obtained the name above every name; that at the mention of His name every knee, in every realm, without exception, will bow and every tongue confess that He is Lord.

No other person was qualified to redeem mankind. Nobody but Jesus had the capability or ability. He voluntarily laid down His life for us, obtained eternal redemption for us, and gave us victory over the devil, sin, the world, and our flesh. When we pray in the name of Jesus, we are enforcing His victory and commanding whatever is in opposition, whether it is sickness, affliction, lack, bondage, and the like, to bow the knee and submit to His authority and victory!

I was introduced to the awesome power in the name of Jesus early on in my Christian walk. Growing up, my father did not go to church. He did not believe in Jesus. My mother would take us to church, but church attendance was more of a religious duty or cultural observance. We did not have a personal relationship with God. My family was involved in ancestral worship, with all its demonic entanglements. Before I became a Christian, I was beginning to dabble in the occult, reading books about hypnosis, spiritism, mediums and so on. I had just started to experiment with these concepts when I gave my life to Christ. When I became a Christian, everything changed! I was severely attacked and oppressed by the demonic spirits I had been exposed to. They did not want me to follow Jesus. Night after night, I would have nightmares with these wicked spirits chasing after me to do me harm. Sometimes, I would be wide awake and sense a demonic presence physically come into the room where I was. I was so scared and my hair would stand on end. At other times, during the night, I would feel these demonic spirits pressing down on me and trying to choke me to death. It was a terrible time! Every night, I would be so afraid to go to sleep. During this time, I began to attend the Assemblies of God church and was in a youth group that was literally on fire for God. I was baptized in the Holy Spirit and learned spiritual warfare. When I shared about the demonic oppression and attacks, they told me to call on the name of Jesus. Nothing prepared me for what happened. When the devil and his minions came to attack and choke me, I would struggle and eventually call forth the name of Jesus. As soon as I spoke His name, they would lose their grip, and take off running! Ultimately, the tables were turned and I completely whipped the demons who had been sent by the devil to kill me. I haven't stopped since! No demon, authority, witch, wizard, medium, psychic or power has the right to oppress a child of God. Just call the name of Jesus and they will flee. Years later, I was able to share the gospel with my father, and lead him to a saving faith in Jesus before he died.

> When we pray in the name of Jesus, we are enforcing His victory and commanding whatever is in opposition to bow to His authority.

The Old Deal

God inaugurated this glorious new deal almost 2000 years ago. But, it is sad to say that so many people are still living under the old deal that is obsolete and set aside. Yes, they proclaim their faith in Christ, but they are still living under the old covenant with its laws and regulations. The hallmark of the old-deal lifestyle is a legalistic approach to relationship with God and people, while the hallmark of the new covenant is a grace-filled approach to our relationship with God and people. John 1:17 states, "For the law was given through Moses, but grace and truth came through Jesus Christ."

Other highlights of the old deal are reliance on good works, church membership, church attendance, acts of service to God and others, sinlessness, Bible reading, prayer/fasting, and other observances to merit or qualify for the goodness of God—His healing, deliverance, provision, protection, salvation, and so on. The old deal often features judgmental attitudes toward people and a wrong view of

God—seeing God as a hard taskmaster or grumpy grandpa waiting to whack people on the head for every infraction.

Under the old-deal mindset, people seek another human being—a pastor, priest, "prayer warrior," or some other person, to pray and intercede between them and God. They point to the example of Abraham's powerful intercession for Lot in Sodom and Gomorrah, and Moses' successful intercession for the Israelites. Abraham and Moses were great men of God, heroes of the faith and great mediators.

> The hallmark of the new covenant is a grace-filled approach to relationship with God and people.

But, their mediation pales in comparison to the Son! Under the new covenant, Jesus is the only mediator. First Timothy 2:5 states, "For there is one God and one mediator between God and man, the man Christ Jesus." This is because, unlike Abraham and Moses, Jesus is the sinless Son of God. His mediation work on the cross is complete, and no human mediator can add to or improve upon what Jesus did. God the Father underscored this point on the Mount of Transfiguration. He, once and for all, publicly declared the supremacy and sole authority of the Son over all, including Moses, representing the law, and Elijah, representing the prophets. Matthew 17:1 reports:

> Now after six days Jesus took Peter, James, and John his brother, led them up on a high mountain by themselves; and He was transfigured before them. His face shone like the sun, and His clothes became as white as the light. And behold, Moses and Elijah appeared to them, talking with Him. Then Peter answered and said to Jesus, "Lord, it is good for us to be here; if You wish, let us make here three

tabernacles: one for You, one for Moses, and one for Elijah." While he was still speaking, behold, a bright cloud overshadowed them; and *suddenly a voice came out of the cloud, saying, "This is My beloved Son, in whom I am well pleased. Hear Him!"*

God is saying, the Son, and only the Son. Jesus lives today to make intercession for us. So, not only did He secure our victory on the cross, he is alive today in the throne room of God, seated at the Father's right hand to enforce that victory.

Perhaps the saddest evidence of an old-deal mindset is an inability to believe in, receive, and truly experience the unconditional love of God. An old-deal mindset is often plagued by guilt, condemnation, and the constant fear of not measuring up or meeting some self or organizationally imposed standard. In contrast, the new deal declares, "There is therefore now no condemnation to those who are in Christ Jesus, who do not walk according to the flesh, but according to the Spirit" (Romans 8:1).

The old deal binds; but the new deal sets free! The old deal looks to me to pay or contribute toward the payment for my sins; the new deal relies exclusively and totally on Christ's lavish payment for me on the cross. The old deal is "me focused"—my sins, works, actions, merits and measurements, whereas the new deal is "God focused" —His love, mercy, forgiveness, and providence. The old deal is bankrupt because of its reliance on man, while the new deal is truly inexhaustible because of its reliance on God and the limitless resources of heaven! Hallelujah!

> *An old deal mindset is often plagued by guilt, condemnation, and the constant fear of not measuring up.*

Hebrews 7: 22–29 sums it up nicely and explains in eloquent detail why the new deal is better than the old, and why the Son, is the only person qualified to guarantee and secure this new covenant. It states:

> Jesus is the one who guarantees this better covenant with God. There were many priests under the old system, for death prevented them from remaining in office. But because Jesus lives forever, His priesthood lasts forever. Therefore, he is able, once and forever, to save those who come to God through Him. He lives forever to intercede with God on their behalf. He is the kind of high priest we need because he is holy and blameless, unstained by sin. He has been set apart from sinners and has been given the highest place of honor in heaven. Unlike those other high priests, he does not need to offer sacrifices every day. They did this for their own sins first and then for the sins of the people. But Jesus did this once for all when he offered Himself as the sacrifice for the people's sins. The law appointed high priests who were limited by human weakness. But after the law was given, God appointed his Son with an oath, and his Son has been made the perfect High Priest forever.

Here again, neither the law, prophets, nor priests under the old covenant were qualified. Nobody else qualifies—nobody but the Son!

When Under Attack

In every attack against you as a son or daughter of God, the devil's goal is to make you question who you are and doubt your identity in Christ. He knows that once you lose your identity as a "son" of God, you go back under the old deal mindset with its wrong view of yourself and God. And when you don't see yourself correctly, you will not see God correctly, and you will not have a right relationship with Him. So, the devil slanders God to you. He says "If God loves you, why are you going through this?" He has all power, He can deliver you, why doesn't He? The goal of the enemy is to get you to distrust God, doubt His love for you, and slip into "self-help" mode. The devil knows that once you step outside the new deal, you will never win. Your only place of victory is in Christ. When you step outside the new covenant in your thinking, then you are no longer relying on the victory of Christ, but facing off against the devil on your own merits. As soon as you take your eyes off Christ, you will see your sin and failure. Now the devil has you on his turf! He will accuse, condemn, oppress, torment and destroy you.

When under attack, sons and daughters of God must run to God and hold on! When your heart is breaking, and you feel abandoned by God, run to Him anyway. Tell Him how you feel, pour out your heart, anguish and tears to Him. When you are in this secret place, bruised, battered, prostrate in pain and worship, you are untouchable by the enemy.

> *When under attack, run to God for safekeeping and abandon yourself to Him.*

The Lord will come to your rescue. Psalms 34:18 states that "The Lord is close to the broken hearted; He rescues those whose spirits are crushed." He will cover you with His wings and shelter you from the storm. He will apply His balm to your wounded heart. He will restore your soul. This is a sacred place, where the enemy cannot follow you in. Jesus modeled this on the cross. He felt abandoned by God, but He did not pull back. Instead, He cried out to God in the words of Psalm 22:1 "My God, My God, why have you abandoned me?" (Matthew 27:46, 50). Then He "released His spirit" to God for safe keeping.

When under attack, run to God for safekeeping and abandon yourself to Him. Believe and rest in His promise that He loves you. He will never leave you or abandon you. The apostle Paul emphasized this truth in 2 Corinthians 4:8-9, when he said, "We are pressed on every side by troubles, but we are not crushed. We are perplexed, but not driven to despair. We are hunted down, but never abandoned by God. We get knocked down, but we are not destroyed."

So, no matter how you feel, you are never alone in your trials. The Lord your God is with you! A critical objective of the devil in every trial that you face, is to convince you that God doesn't love you. In Romans 8:35-39 (KJV), apostle Paul asks "Who shall separate us from the love of Christ?" and then he proceeds to list things like, trouble, tribulation, distress, famine, persecution, danger, and so on.

There is a "who" behind the "what" of life's troubles.

Years ago, when I looked at the problems he listed, I thought to myself that the right question should have been, "What can separate us from the love of God?" But God spoke to my heart and said "behind the what, there is a who." We see the "what" and we focus on the "what" of life's troubles, but apostle Paul under the inspiration of the Holy Spirit, wanted us to know that there is a "who" behind the "what" of life's troubles. It is the devil, and his entire objective is to destroy our confidence in God's love for us. The physical problems are merely his means to that end. Do not let him win!

Proclamation

I am a son/daughter of God. I am an heir of God and a joint heir with Christ. Because of Jesus's sacrifice for me, I refuse to surrender my identity as a child of God. I refuse to hang my head and walk in shame, regret or live in the past. I refuse to cower in fear, or linger in self-doubt. I refuse to answer to any labels, limits or stereotypes that any man or woman may want to place on me. I break out of every box of human definition. I look sickness, poverty, divorce, failure and rejection in the eye and declare, I belong to God and I answer to only one label, title and name – Son/daughter of Almighty God! Amen.

> *Before I was born, before I had a chance to do good or bad, God loved me, chose me in Christ, and decided to adopt me into His family.*

STUDY QUESTIONS

1. What is the new deal? How does it impact your relationship with God? Are you part of the new deal? If not, how can you become a part of it?

2. Why is Jesus our only access to God? Discuss the pressure by society to be tolerant of other faiths claiming to provide access to God. What is the Bible's response?

3. Why is walking as sons of God our only portal to the supernatural power of God? Discuss Galatians 4:1–7.

4. What are the finished works of Christ? List and discuss all that Jesus did for us on the cross. How can you appropriate them? What is your role in bringing them into manifestation in your life?

5. Do you qualify for God's blessings, salvation, favor, healing, provision, grace, goodness, or deliverance? How?

6. What is a power of attorney? What type of power of attorney did Jesus give all believers? How can we use that authority in our daily lives?

7. Are you walking as a "son" of God under the new covenant? Are there vestiges of the old deal in your approach to God and people? Pray in the spirit and ask Holy Spirit to direct your self-examination. Ask Him to show you where there are gaps or where you are mixing the old and the new. Make a

decision today to walk in the grace and truth of the new covenant!

8. 8. What is the right way to respond when you are under attack?

SONSHIP

Abba Father is the distinct cry of the Spirit of the Son. This is a bold cry, a cry of sonship, love, relationship, dependence, trust, expectancy, and reliance. God always hears the cry of the Spirit of His Son! The cry of fear, worry, anxiety, self-pity, powerlessness, and so on, is not the cry of the Spirit of Jesus. It is a strange cry.

CHAPTER 2
A PORTRAIT OF NEW COVENANT SONSHIP

Fatherhood is a central and dominant theme in the Bible. The reason is simple. God is a father! In scripture, there are many different names used to describe God. While all the names of God are significant and very important in their meaning and revelation of the character of God, the name Abba Father is perhaps the most tender of all because it identifies the special, close, intimate relationship of a father and His beloved child. Jesus taught us to call God Abba Father, or Daddy. Before Jesus came, God's name was unspeakable, and the Israelites would not even call God by His name. Under the old covenant, God was fearsome, and the relationship of people to God was that of master and servant. Then Jesus came and inaugurated the new covenant, a personal relationship and affinity with God.

God is still as fearsome, high, lofty, holy, and exalted as he always was, but now he is also a daddy—our daddy! What a paradigm shift. You see, a great king can be fearsome to all his subjects, but to his son, he is not fearsome at all. He is daddy! He did not change or lose any of his power or prestige. But that power is colored by and seen through the lens of relationship, affinity, and tender love. When we become born again, we are adopted into God's family. A key outcome of that legal transaction is a new relationship where God deals with us as His beloved children.

Ephesians 1:5 states: "God decided in advance to adopt us into his own family by bringing us to Himself through Jesus Christ. This is what he wanted to do, and it gave Him great pleasure."

In today's world, a dad who just had a new addition to his family, either by birth or adoption, will tell family and friends and post photos on social media to announce the happy event. Ephesians 1:5 tells us that Father God was overjoyed at our new birth into His family. So, the first thing he does is to celebrate and spread the word! He throws a party in heaven, and the angels rejoice. He then sends His Holy Spirit into our hearts as a herald of our adoption and new relationship status.

Romans 8:15–17 states:

> For you did not receive the spirit of bondage again to fear, but you received the Spirit of adoption by whom we cry out, "Abba, Father." The Spirit Himself bears witness with our spirit that we are children of God and if children, then heirs—heirs of God and joint heirs with Christ, if indeed we suffer with Him, that we may also be glorified together.

Immediately upon our salvation, an impartation takes place. God deposits in us a piece of Himself, His Spirit. The Holy Spirit is God's imprimatur, His signature or mark identifying us as His own. The Holy Spirit moves into our hearts with a joyful announcement of our new birth into the family of God. He confirms our identity as children of God and partakers of His divine nature. He deposits God's seed, the Word, containing His DNA and divine nature into us! (2 Peter 1:3–4). First Peter 1:23 explains: "having been born again, not of corruptible seed but incorruptible, through the Word of God which lives and abides forever."

> *The Holy Spirit deposits God's seed, the Word, containing His DNA and divine nature into us.*

The Holy Spirit is called the Spirit of adoption because He confirms and makes real to us this great legal trans- action of adoption. How does He do that? By working in two directions: one by bringing God's fatherly love to us and the other by bringing our childlike affections for God. "He does this by replacing the fear of a slave toward a master with the love of a son toward a father. 'You did not receive the spirit of slavery to fall back into fear, but you have received the Spirit of adoption as sons, by whom we cry, "Abba! Father!"' He is contrasting the fear of a slave with the affection of a son. The work of the Holy Spirit in our lives is to change our slavish fears toward God into confident, happy, peaceful affection for God as our father" (John Piper, *Desiring God*).

Romans 5:5 states, "Hope does not disappoint because the love of God has been poured out within our hearts through the Holy Spirit who was given to us" John Piper explains, "God's love for His children – is poured out in our hearts through the Holy Spirit. This is the Spirit of adoption making real to us the love of our Father, applying it to us so that we know that we are loved. He makes the truth of our acceptance and the value of our Father real to us and pours out the love of the Father into our lives (Romans 5:5). We enjoy emotionally the Fatherhood of God by the testimony of the Spirit.

The witness of the Holy Spirit that we are children of God is the creation in us of affections for God. The testimony of the Holy Spirit *is* the cry, "Abba! Father!" And the reason Paul uses the word *cry* and the Aramaic word *Abba* is because both of them point to deep, affectionate, personal, authentic experience of God's fatherly love" (Piper).

Abba Father is the distinct cry of the Spirit of the Son. This is a bold cry, a cry of sonship, love, relationship, dependence, trust, expectancy, and reliance. God always hears the cry of the Spirit of His Son! The cry of fear, worry, anxiety, self-pity, powerlessness, and so on, is not the cry of the Spirit of Jesus. It is a strange cry.

Becoming a child of God is the highest and most humbling of honors. Because of it, we have a new relationship with God and a new standing before Him. Instead of running from God and trying to hide our sin like Adam and Eve did, we run to Him calling, "Abba Father" and finding grace and forgiveness in Christ.

> *Abba Father is the distinct cry of the Spirit of the Son.*

Jesus taught us to pray, "Our Father in heaven, hallowed be your name" (Matthew 6:9). Being an adopted child of God is the source of our hope, the security of our future, and the motivation to live a life "worthy of the calling you have received" (Ephesians 4:1). This realization evokes only one logical response from grateful hearts—praise! Our hearts cry, "our Father in heaven, hallowed be your name!"

Sonship Mandate

Sonship is the birthright, purpose, and destiny of every child of God. Our sonship mandate describes our authorization from our Father to become like Him. It is our official commission, order, injunction, and directive to manifest the qualities, abilities, and capabilities of God in the earth. God is our source, and our mandate originates from Him.

In Genesis 1:26 God said:

Let us make man in our image, according to our likeness and let them have dominion over the fish of the sea, and the birds of the air and over the cattle and over all of the earth and every creeping thing that creeps on the earth. God created man in his own image, in the image of God he created him. Male and female he created them.

In Genesis 1, we see a pattern. When God wanted to create anything, he spoke to the source of the thing. In verse 11 God said: "Let the land sprout with vegetation. . . . And it was so." In verse 20 God said, "Let the waters swarm with fish and other life . . . and . . . Let the skies be filled with birds of every kind. . . . And it was so." In verse 24, God said, "Let the earth bring forth every sort of animal. . . And it was so." The pattern is, God speaks to the source of the thing to be created to bring forth and it brought forth. When it came time to make man, God spoke to Himself. He said, "Let us make man in our image, according to our likeness." God is our source of origin, not tadpoles, a big bang, or anything else. Mankind came from God. We are His offspring (Acts 17:28).

God reproduced us after His kind—the god kind. We are like God, having His attributes, nature and capable of manifesting His power. First John 4:17(b) KJV states that as He, Jesus, is, so are we in this world. We are made in the image and likeness of God. An image is an authentic representation of a person or thing and likeness is the capacity to resemble, replicate, or reproduce that person or thing.

> *God reproduced us after His kind—the god kind. We are like God, having His attributes, nature and capable of manifesting His power.*

We are an authentic representation of God in the earth and have the capacity to reproduce Him, His love, character, grace, and so forth on the earth. This is why Colossians 3:17, instructs us as follows, "And whatever you do or say, do it as a representative of the Lord Jesus".

In Psalm 8, David ponders this awesome truth and marvels that God made human beings after the god kind—only just a little lower than Himself and delegated to us authority over all of creation. He asks rhetorically:

> What are mere mortals that you should think about them, human beings that you should care for them? Yet you made them only a little lower than God and crowned them with glory and honor. You gave them charge of everything you made, putting all things under their authority—the flocks and the herds and all the wild animals, the birds in the sky, the fish in the sea, and everything that swims the ocean currents. O Lord, our Lord, your majestic name fills the earth!

God our Father wants us to walk in the rights, authority and privileges of sonship. This was His express intent, plan, and purpose. He wanted us to occupy and rule over the earth, acting in His stead, as God. He has no limits, and because He is our source of authority, we can live life without limits.

The mission of the Holy Spirit in our lives is to help us to understand the full meaning and implications of sonship, establish our destiny and birthright as "sons" of God, and empower us to walk in the privileges and rights of sonship. The ultimate goal of God is to enable us to follow and reproduce the pattern—Jesus is the pattern Son. God wants every Christian to grow and mature from children into sonship until we look like Jesus in word and deed.

In Luke 3:38 the Bible declares that Adam was "the son of God." That was His original mandate. But mankind lost our sonship mandate due to the sin of Adam. But the last Adam, Jesus Christ, who was both the Son of man and the Son of God, restored us to sonship. Once we receive Jesus, we are restored as "sons" of God. As John 1:12 states: "But as many as received him, to them he gave the power to become the sons of God, even to those who believe in his name."

> God wants us to occupy and rule over the earth, acting in His stead, as God.

Part of our sonship mandate is to rule as kings and priests on the earth. Speaking of the sons and daughters of God, Revelation 5:10 says of Jesus: "For You were slain, and have redeemed us to God by Your blood out of every tribe and tongue and people and nation, and have made us kings and priests to our God; And we shall reign on the earth."

First Peter 2:9 echoes this truth as it says of the "sons" of God, "You are a chosen generation, a royal priesthood, a holy nation, a peculiar people." The kingly anointing is the anointing of authority and the priestly anointing is the anointing of power. God has imbued us with this dual anointing for the express purpose of empowering us to reign on the earth. With this scripture in mind, isn't it amazingly flawed and limiting how much stock we put on fitting in and how much resources we expend in trying to accomplish that objective? We are not called to fit in. We are called to rule the planet!

God has given us both the power to become "sons" of God and the pattern or model of sonship to emulate. Your manifestation as a "son" is a gift you give both yourself, those who interact with you and all of creation. Romans 8:19 states: "For the creation waits in eager expectation for the manifestation of the sons of God." All of creation is waiting eagerly for you and me to step into and fulfill our sonship mandate. Because through our operation as sons, "the creation itself will be liberated from its bondage to decay and brought into the freedom and glory of the children of God" (Romans 8:21). All of creation is waiting on you and me to manifest as "sons" of God! Why? Because sonship confers on us the authority and ability to liberate all of creation from bondage. This means that when we choose to remain children, we maintain the bondage on all of creation.

> *We are not called to fit in. We are called to rule the planet!*

Ecclesiastes 10:17 describes this vividly: "Woe to you, O land, when your king is a child, And your princes feast in the morning! Blessed are you, O land, when your king is the son of nobles, and your princes feast at the proper time; for strength and not for drunkenness!"

The Devil's Identity Theft

"Identity Theft is Skyrocketing, and Getting More Sophisticated". This was the headline of a February 27, 2018 article by MarketWatch. The report states: "We've heard about the identity theft epidemic for so long that many have become numb to the news, and the large numbers – 50 million stolen credit cards here, 150 million in stolen Social Security numbers there. But this is no time for complacency. There were two bits of very bad news for consumers in the recent annual survey of identity-based fraud. First, there were 16.7 million victims in 2017, easily the most for all time, fueled in part by a series of high-profile data breaches. But even worse, criminals are migrating to more sophisticated, multi-step frauds, with the rates of new account fraud and non-credit card fraud soaring. Why should you care? Those are the crimes with the most potential to hurt your credit score."

The article proceeds to describe how one in fifteen people were victims of identity theft in 2017. Sobering! This type of information chills you to the bone. But it is nothing compared to the devil's identity theft. The enemy has launched an all-out offensive against the body of Christ, and the stakes are so much higher than the physical identity theft. Our eternal souls, as well as the plans and purposes of God for planet earth hang in the balance. Also, like the human criminals, the devil is getting more sophisticated and executing multi-step frauds to dupe Christians and steal their identity, authority and power. Like the article says, "This is no time for complacency." Rather, it's time to unmask the enemy and expose his strategy!

Marks of New Covenant Sonship

There are two key marks of new covenant sonship:

1. Identity: This gives you the right, authority and sense of belonging. In the natural world, your identity and self-definition come from your father. He determines your gender and gives you his last name, as a mark of ownership and belonging. You belong to his family! Likewise, for spiritual sonship, our identity and self-definition come from our origin or source, our heavenly Father. John 1:12 (KJV) states, "But

as many as received Him, to them gave He power to become the sons of God, even to them that believe on His name." He gives us His name and identity, and seals us with the Holy Spirit to confirm that we are His. We belong to His family!

> *A loss of identity results in a loss of equality and shuts down access to the resources and inheritance of the Father.*

2. Equality: Our identity as "sons" of God, give us equality with Christ and access to the resources and inheritance of our Father, God. Romans 8:17 states, "And if sons, then heirs—heirs of God and joint heirs with Christ." A loss of identity, results in a loss of equality and shuts down access to the resources and inheritance of the Father.

When you know your identity, you are secure in the affirmation of your Father and can confidently partake in your inheritance. On the other hand, if you do not know your identity, the devil can rob you of your inheritance as a "son" of God.

The Devil's Multi-Step ID Theft Strategy

A major challenge for men and women who have been or are going through severe trials, is how to overcome the devil's attack against their identity, authority and sense of belonging as "sons" of God. Here is the devil's multi-step identity theft strategy, not necessarily in any chronological order:

1. First, the enemy attacks your security and rest in Christ. He plays on your human need to understand and make sense of

what happened. His favorite questions begin with why and where? Why did you go through this and where is God when you need Him?

2. Then, he challenges and questions your trust in God. How can you trust God? If He stood by and allowed these traumatic circumstances to come into your life, how can you trust him to protect you?

3. Next, he plagues your heart with fear! If God allowed that to happen to you, what else might He allow? He tells you, "you are on your own and anything can happen to you."

4. Then, he attacks your faith and sows doubt and unbelief. When you pray, the enemy reminds you of how you prayed in the other situation and nothing happened. When you attempt to believe a bible verse, and stand on it in faith, he reminds you how you did the same thing before and it didn't work.

5. Next, he mocks your prayer life. What is the point of prayer anyway? Look how much you pray, and for what? Is your life any better than the lives of those who don't pray as much or at all? Look at your other relative who is not a Christian, her life is great, and she has none of your problems.

6. Then, he accuses you. You are a terrible sinner. There must be something you did to bring this upon yourself. If it isn't God's fault, then it must be yours. He then quotes the bible to you, sometimes through misguided Christians – "you reap what you sow" (Galatians 6:7). So, you must have sowed this.

7. Next, he questions the faithfulness of God to His promises. God doesn't keep His word. Look at all the promises and prophetic words you received and believed in faith, all to no avail!

8. Then he derides your ability to hear from God and incites confusion. When you listen and believe that you are hearing the voice of God and want to respond in obedience, the devil shows up and asks you how you can be sure, really sure? After all, you thought you heard from God that other time too and the outcome was bad. You were wrong then, how do you know that you are right this time?

9. Next, he challenges and tries to silence your witness and testimony. Look at your life, he snickers, it is a mess. How dare you speak to another person about God? What do you have to say? Your life is a reproach, who will listen to you anyway? Simply shut up!

10. Then he questions God's love for you. God doesn't love you. If He did, why are you going through this? God can deliver you, why doesn't He? Think about it, if it were your son or daughter, would you let him or her go through this if you can stop it? God doesn't care. He delights in seeing you suffer and wants to grind you into the dust.

11. Next, he exploits the time element. This situation has lingered for so long and remained unchanged for days, months and years, despite your many prayers and faith. Why subject yourself to continued pressure, shame, embarrassment, and the crushing pain of repeated disappointment? It hurts too much to hope and believe again, only to be disappointed again and again. Just give up!

12. Finally, he goes for the foundation. He attacks the word of God. Since that scripture or promise of God that you have been standing on for so long did not come to pass, then the word of God is not true, the bible is a farce and none of this is for real.

This is a devastating cycle of attacks, and the devil is unrelenting in bombarding your mind with these thoughts. His strategy is extremely effective if the situation has lingered for a long time. Over time, sustained pressure on many sides and repeated disappointment can pile up, wear down a Christian and make him or her more vulnerable. The enemy's goal is to steal your identity and equality, and in so doing, your access to God's resources. He wants to render you ineffective and impotent as a Christian, and ultimately, to drive you to hopelessness and despair. He wants you to be like the men and women that apostle Paul described in 2 Timothy 3:5, as "Having a form of godliness, but denying the power thereof". You see, the devil doesn't mind you going to church and serving diligently, as long as you live in defeat and there is no evidence in your life that you walk with Christ. This outcome achieves a two-fold objective for the enemy. First, he can discredit God as a bad Father, and if someone else wants to become a Christian, he can point to you and ask them in disdain, "do you want to be like him or her?"

Pathway to Victory

Romans 8:31-39 outlines our response to the devil's attacks and gives us a pathway to victory. It tells us to talk back to the devil and gives us what to say. Even if you are still struggling to believe the word of God, do not understand what is going on and cannot see or explain God's workings in your life, you can trust His heart and talk back to the devil with confidence:

1. God is for me. Tell the devil over and over again, God is for me. I don't know why I am going through this, but one thing I know, God is for me. He is not against me. I am not in this by myself. God is for me (Romans 8:31).

2. God is not holding out on me. When I was still a sinner and an enemy of God, He gave me Jesus, the best that heaven had. If He gave me Jesus, why would He withhold healing, finances, breakthrough, and so on, from me? God loves me, He will never hold out on me (Romans 8:32).

3. God chose me in Christ to be His child, devil, how dare you accuse me? God justified me and gave me right standing with Himself. I reject every voice of accusation and judgement (Romans 8:33).

4. No one can condemn me. Satan, I rebuke you! There is no condemnation for me, because I am in Christ Jesus. Every tongue that rises against me in judgement, I condemn (Isaiah 54:17b). Jesus is sitting at the right hand of God right now, speaking up for me (Romans 8:34).

5. God loves me. Our best response to the devil's lies that God doesn't love us, because he allowed trouble in our lives, is found in Romans 8:35-37. It states:

> "Can anything ever separate us from Christ's love? Does it mean He no longer loves us if we have trouble or calamity, or are persecuted, or hungry, or destitute, or in danger, or threatened with death? As the Scriptures say, "For your sake we are killed every

day; we are being slaughtered like sheep." No, despite all these things, overwhelming victory is ours through Christ, who loved us.

6. I don't need to understand. Right now, I don't understand and can't explain what God is doing in my life, but I trust Him. I know that He is working on my behalf. Somehow, He will make all this work together for my good.

7. Regardless, I will wait on the Lord. I will stay upon His word. I will serve, and I will worship. I believe the word of God that this situation is working for me. So, I fix my eyes, not on what I see, but on what is unseen, because what I see is temporal, meaning that it is subject to change, but what is unseen is eternal (2 Corinthians 4:18). Even if this situation on earth does not change, my eternal future is secure in Christ. I know the end of my story, and I win!

8. Declare Romans 8:38-39, proclaiming your victory in Christ!

> And I am convinced that nothing can ever separate me from God's love. Neither death nor life, neither angels nor demons, neither my fears for today nor my worries about tomorrow—not even the powers of hell can separate me from God's love. No power in the sky above or in the earth below—indeed, nothing in all creation will ever be able to separate me from the love of God that is revealed in Christ Jesus my Lord."

Proclamation

I am a son/daughter of God. I am an heir of God and a joint-heir with Christ. I take authority over every attack of the devil against me and my family. I shut down and cancel every plan of the devil to steal, kill and destroy in my life. The counsel of the enemy shall not stand. No weapon formed against me shall prosper and every tongue that rises against me in judgment, I condemn. I declare that it is well with me in Jesus name. I reverse every orchestration launched by the devil against me and my family. I shut down his operation of failure, defeat and destruction and replace it with victory, increase, restoration and overflow! Amen.

STUDY QUESTIONS

1. Why is the name Abba such a special name for God? What are some of the wrong views of God that people have? Why is it hard for some people to relate to God as a loving Father? Discuss your experiences and testimonies that illustrate the fatherhood of God in your lives.

2. Discuss and review the role of the Holy Spirit in our lives. Who is He? What are His characteristics, and why is He called the Spirit of Adoption? As a group, pool your Bible knowledge and discuss Bible stories that reinforce the role of the Holy Spirit in our salvation and relationship with God.

3. What is the impartation that takes place immediately upon our salvation, and what does God deposit in us? What does that deposit represent? Thank God for the ministry of the Holy Spirit in your life.

4. What is our sonship mandate? When was this mandate initiated by God? How can we demonstrate and execute this mandate in our lives?

5. The Bible says that we are reproduced after the God kind. What does that mean? How can we operate like God on the earth? What can we learn from the example of Jesus?

6. Using dictionaries and reference books, discuss the distinction between power and authority? God has called us to be kings and priests on the earth. Pool your Bible knowledge and name kings and priests in the Bible. Discuss

and review how they exercised their power and authority. How can we reign as kings on the earth?

7. How can we walk in the privileges and rights of sonship? As a group, name and discuss Bible characters who walked in the rights and authority of sonship. What can we learn from them?

8. What are the devil's identity theft strategies and what is our pathway to victory? As a group, share personal testimonies of times when you were attacked by the devil. How did you overcome?

> *Our sonship mandate is our authorization from our Father to become like Him.*

SONSHIP PRINCIPLES

The Word of God coming out of my mouth, in faith, is the most potent weapon known to man. What this means, is that every word I speak is on assignment. Once I believe the Word in my heart and launch it forth via the spoken word, it will not return empty; it will achieve its creative purpose and assignment. It is unstoppable!

CHAPTER 3
SEVEN POWERFUL PRINCIPLES ON HOW TO WALK AS A "SON" OF GOD IN THE EARTH

PRINCIPLE 1: You Have Great Value!

God has placed tremendous value in us—He calls us sons and daughters! I am a son or daughter of Almighty God. I am an heir of God and a joint heir with Christ. I have the DNA of God. I am a partaker of His divine nature. I have the mind of Christ. I am of inestimable value. The value of a thing is measured by how much people are willing to pay for it. Jesus gave His life for me—that defines my value as a son or daughter of God.

I must recognize my personal value and own it. Self-talk is very important because it outlines the image of myself that I have on the inside. My self-image is critical because what I believe and say about myself has the greatest impact on my life more than any other person's words spoken over me. As a son or daughter of God, I must be able to say to myself with deep conviction, "I have something of great value to offer others—myself and who I am in Christ."

I win in life only when I recognize and embrace my personal value in Christ. Winners say I CAN. That confidence comes from a deeper I AM. For a believer, that confidence comes from who I am and whose I am. I belong to God. I am a son or daughter of Almighty God. I am seated

> *I win in life only when I recognize and embrace my personal value in Christ.*

in heavenly places in Christ Jesus. All things are possible to me because I believe. I AM SO I CAN. Philippians 4:13 (AMP) puts it succinctly: "I can do all things through Him who strengthens *and* empowers me. I am self-sufficient in Christ's sufficiency; I am ready for anything and equal to anything through Him who infuses me with inner strength and confident peace." This is the winners creed, and it begins with I *can*. Conversely, losers say: *I don't think I can*. That lack of confidence, hesitation, and self-doubt comes from a deeper *I don't think I am*. This is why the devil works so hard to attack, steal, or distort our identity in Christ.

My value comes from my source. It does not come from my performance, whether or not people like me, how much money I have, my net worth, who I know, what I drive, how I look, and so on. God is my source of origin, and that source will never diminish in value. So, nothing and no one can truly devalue me. In his book, *25 Ways to Win with People,* John Maxwell provided a vivid illustration. A $100 bill may be crumpled, tossed on the ground, stepped on, and ground into the dust. But it will never lose its value. It is still a $100 bill and legal tender for goods and services regardless of how dirty or crumpled it is. The same analogy is applicable to us as human beings. We may be dropped, crumpled, ground into the dust, and dirtied by life, but that will never devalue us because our value comes from God, our creator, not from our status, circumstances, or the approval or opinion of other people.

I must believe in my personal value with such conviction that I will *not* settle for less than what God has for me. I have heard it said that in life, you don't get what you deserve but what you are able and willing to negotiate for. This is why people with low self-image, who don't believe in and own their personal value, lose again and again. They always negotiate against themselves. Because they don't believe that they are valuable, they don't negotiate hard enough for what they want. When pressure sets in, they cave in and settle for less out of fear that they may lose out altogether.

> *I must believe in my personal value with such conviction that I will not settle for less than what God has for me.*

In 2001, I was working at Enron Corporation in Houston, Texas. On December 5, Enron went bankrupt, and I lost my job, 401K, benefits and more. I lost it all, along with 5000 other employees. Earlier, in October, the Lord had invited me into a time of fasting and prayer. During the fast, Enron's financial problems hit the fan, and I became aware of them. I cried to the Lord and He gave me a Word. He said, "For others, the fall of Enron will be a casting down, but for you, it will be a lifting up." After Enron fell, I was invited for interview by Conectiv Energy and was offered a job in March. Just as the Lord had said, my starting pay at Conectiv Energy was twenty five thousand dollars more than my salary at Enron. But here is the personal value illustration. I requested a sign-on bonus! Think about it! I had been out of a job for a couple months, was in the job market with 5000 other people desperately looking for "just anything." Conectiv Energy knew I was out of a job, so one could say that I had no leverage. However, I knew my God and what He had said to me. I refused to accept the job without a sign-on bonus. The hiring manager told me that he would have to receive approval from his superiors to authorize a sign-on bonus. So, I traveled back to Houston! All the way back to Houston, the devil drummed in my ear.

Are you crazy? You don't have a job and have been out of a job for a few months in a job market flooded with former Enron employees, many of whom are better qualified that you. Call them back and take the job as is. If not, they may offer it to another person. To make matters worse, I knew many of my former Enron colleagues were taking lower paying jobs just to have a job, and here God has given me a great job, at a director level, with a twenty five thousand dollar salary increase. Fear screamed at me, "Take the job now." But I knew God's word is true. I was there on His ticket, not mine. He opened this door, and nobody can shut it. I was not willing to leave anything on the table that God had prepared for me. So, I held on to the Word of God and went back home. Well, the next week, the company called and paid me a twelve thousand dollar sign-on bonus! Why was I able to hold out and negotiate for more? It was because I knew whose I was and what God had told me. I knew that I was precious to God and that He would keep His promise. So, I owned my personal value and refused to settle for less! To God's glory, I went on to excel marvelously in that job and was a tremendous asset to the company.

I am a very valuable person. So is every son and daughter of God! I don't spend my time trying to convince people of my value. Jesus already did that. I simply own it. Believing in my personal value keeps me from discounting myself or selling myself short. My time is valuable. So, I do not spend my time or give myself to people who don't value me. Jesus paid the full price for me. I will not give myself away at a discount!

Owning my personal value allows me to be authentic. God wants me to be authentic. He made me an original. I must be comfortable in my own skin. I am an uncommon package, with my personality, quirks, skin color, ethnicity, and so forth. I was uniquely put together by God and assigned a unique identifier—my fingerprint. I am one of a kind. Nothing about me is an accident.

Authenticity is God's permission to be what He designed me to be. Authenticity gives me personal authority. If you try to be someone else, you will have no genuine authority and will not succeed because you are not being true to who you are. Like Joyce Meyer said, "You might as well be yourself because everybody else is taken." Authenticity allows me to be the best me that I can be. It celebrates difference, so I should celebrate my difference. When I embrace my personal value and authenticity, the anointing of God is dispensed through me to change and impact my world.

This is what happened with Moses. When God called him to lead the Israelites out of Egypt, he did not recognize, believe in, or own his personal value. He lamented his deficiencies and produced a string of objections, each detailing why he was not the man for the job (Exodus 3 and 4; NLT). He had such a low self-image. First, he said, "Who am I to appear before Pharaoh? Who am I to lead the people of Israel out of Egypt?" Then he said, "What if they won't believe me, or listen to me?" Next, he said, "I'm not very good with words, I get tongue tied and my words get tangled." Finally, in desperation, he said, "Lord, please send anyone else." Moses forgot that God knew exactly who he was and the package he came in. When he complained about his speaking ability, God asked him "Who makes a person's mouth? Who decides whether people speak or do not speak, hear or do not hear, see or do not see? It is not I, the Lord?" It took some doing, but God finally convinced Moses to go to Egypt and lead the people of Israel out. When he embraced his personal value and authenticity, the anointing of God was dispensed through him to change the world and impact history. His quirks, speech impediment, and other limitations were no match or barrier for the power of Almighty God. The same Moses went down in history as one of the greatest leaders the world has ever known and a man God called His friend.

> *Owning my personal value allows me to be authentic, and authenticity gives me personal authority.*

If you have been through a traumatic experience, and the devil is challenging your identity and self-worth, do not surrender your sense of personal value to him! Do not accept a spirit of shame, reproach and humiliation. Lift up your head! Read the Bible, believe that you are who God says that you are, and can do what God says that you can do. Say aloud to yourself, regardless of how you feel "I can do it, because the Bible says I can."

PRINCIPLE 2: God Our Father Gave Us the Power to Become "Sons" of God

When we receive Jesus as Savior, God gives us the power to become "sons" of God (John 1:12 KJV). This does not mean that we all become male or try to look or act like men. New covenant sonship is gender neutral. What it does mean is that we, as sons and daughters of God, have the ability, potential, and opportunity to grow into maturity and operate in the authority and power of sonship. Children have authority, dominion, and power. "Sons" exercise authority, dominion, and power. "Sons" rule! Simply stated, mature sons and daughters of God deploy and actualize their right to govern and exercise power in the earth.

The Bible says in Romans 5:17 that those who have received an abundance of grace and the gift of righteousness will reign in life through Christ. That describes every child of God—we all have received from God, an abundance of grace and the gift of righteousness. But sadly "reign in life" is not the reality or testimony of most children of God. Growth into sonship enables us to actualize this inheritance and make it real in our daily experience.

In Revelation 5:10, the Bible says that God has made us kings and priests, and we shall reign on the earth. As noted earlier, the kingly anointing is the anointing of authority and the priestly anointing is the anointing of power. This scripture is saying that God has given us the anointing, authority and power, to reign and rule in the earth.

> God has given us the anointing, authority and power, to reign and rule in the earth.

Delegated Authority

God has all power but has delegated authority over the earth to mankind. We have power, authority, right, liberty, jurisdiction, strength, and ability over the earth. To put it bluntly, God is not in control of the earth; we are or should be because God placed us in authority, gave us the right to rule the planet as "sons" of God, and gave us the free will to choose to exercise that right.

This delegation of authority was not an afterthought. It was God's express intent, which He initiated at creation. In the first five days of creation, God made the heavens and the earth, and filled them. Then, on the sixth day, he created mankind and put us in charge. Genesis 2:19–20 states that God made animals, birds, and every living creature and brought them to the man to see what he would call them, and whatsoever the man called every living creature, that became its name. God gave man the right and authority to name all creation. God put man in charge, right from the beginning!

Sometimes, I hear people lament the evil in the world and ask in a pained voice, "Why doesn't God do something about it?" Some even use the evil in the world as their evidence for the nonexistence of God. They say, if God exists, how can a good God allow such rampant evil? Well, here is your answer. God is not responsible for the calamity, evil, depravity, and utter mayhem on the earth. Mankind is. We are in charge of the earth and wreak pain and devastation by the choices we make and actions we take. We can stop the devastation at any time by making different choices. Romans 6:16 explains: "Don't you realize that you become the slave of whatever you choose to obey? You can be a slave to sin, which leads to death, or you can choose to obey God, which leads to righteous living." God made us like Himself and will not violate our free will to choose to do right or wrong.

Genesis 2:7, 21-23 states:

> Then the Lord God formed the man from the dust of the ground. He breathed the breath of life into the man's nostrils, and the man became a living person. In verse 21–23, we read: "So, the Lord God caused the man to fall into a deep sleep. While the man slept, the Lord God took out one of the man's ribs and closed up the opening. Then the Lord God made a woman from the rib, and he brought her to the man. "At last!" the man exclaimed. "This one is bone from my bone, and flesh from my flesh! She will be called 'woman,' because she was taken from 'man.'"

God gave the man and woman a body so that they could function and interact with the earth. Even though man is a spirit, he lives in a body, an "earth suit" so that he can administer and oversee the earth. Man needed a body to fulfill his God-given assignment to rule the earth, so God gave man a body. Spirits were not put in charge of the earth. Spirits do not have bodies and do not have authority in the earth. Only beings with an "earth suit" have authority on this planet. Spirits can only exercise authority on the earth through entities with flesh and blood. This is why, when God wanted to intervene in the earth, he had to take on flesh and blood. God became a man!

What this means is that Satan, as a spirit, has no authority in the earth. He has to act through the agency of entities with flesh and blood. So, the only authority he has in the earth is the authority we give him. This is why the devil's chief strategy against mankind is deception! Through lies, stratagems, trickery, subterfuge, and cunning, the devil works to steal mankind's authority in the earth or deceive us into surrendering it to him. Jesus warned us about this. In John 8:44, He told us plainly that the devil "has always hated the truth, because there is no truth in him. When he lies, he speaks his native language; for he is a liar and the father of lies."

> Satan, as a spirit, has no authority in the earth. The only authority he has is the authority we give him.

Where Does the Devil Get His Power?

Lucifer was an archangel. His angelic power was subject to the direction and authority of God. When he rebelled against God, he lost his authority. So, he cannot legitimately use angelic power to operate in the earth. Also, he is a spirit and does not have authority in the earth. To operate in the earth, he needs a body. So, the devil's power is the power of deception, to beguile entities with bodies and get them to come under his control and do his bidding.

In Hebrews 3:13 (Amp) the Bible states:

> But instead warn, admonish, urge and encourage one another every day, as long as it is called Today, that none of you may be hardened into settled rebellion by the deceitfulness of sin, by the fraudulence, the stratagem, the trickery which the delusive glamour of sin may play on him.

In John 10:10, Jesus explains: "The thief comes only to steal, and kill and destroy. I came that they may have and enjoy life and have it in abundance, to the full, till it overflows."

So, we learn from the Word of God that the devil is a liar and a thief. He is a fraudster, strategist, and trickster. His first move is to lie. If you believe or engage his lie, he proceeds to steal, and then he can kill and destroy. He is a thief. What does he want to steal? The Word of God, your authority, and your identity in Christ. But he starts with a lie. In Genesis 3:1, he said to Eve "Did God really say you must not eat the fruit from any of the trees in the garden?" Then when Eve engaged him, he lied to her "You won't die!' the serpent replied to the woman. God knows that your eyes will be opened as soon as you eat it, and you will be like God, knowing both good and evil." Unfortunately, Eve believed his lie and ate the fruit. By that sinful act, she ceded her authority to the devil and became a slave to him. Once he stole her authority, then he moved in to kill and destroy her life, relationship with God and family.

How Do We Empower the Devil?

First Peter 5:8 gives us a clue. It warns: "Stay alert! Watch out for your great enemy, the devil. He prowls around like a roaring lion, looking for someone to devour." Several key points emerge from this scripture:

First, we are engaged in an ongoing spiritual battle and there is a grave need for vigilance. We must be alert, because our enemy the devil, is a strategist, trickster and illusionist, and deception is a prime tool of his trade. We stay alert when we are focused on the Word of God and refuse to be distracted, hoodwinked or seduced by the devil.

> *We are engaged in an ongoing spiritual battle and there is a grave need for vigilance.*

Second, the devil is our great enemy. He may try through various disguises and personas, to persuade or deceive us into thinking that he is our friend and that his ideas and proposals stem from his care for our wellbeing, but that is a lie. When he told Eve, "God knows that your eyes will be opened as soon as you eat it, and you will be like God, knowing both good and evil" you would think that he was looking out for Eve, but it was all a lie. The only truth about the devil, is that he is a liar and the father of lies (John 8:44).

A favorite strategy of the devil is to get us to make enemies out of each other and fight, accuse and devour one another. He is "the accuser of the brethren" (Revelations 12:10 KJV), and loves to enlist Christians to do his work. The Bible warns us about that. In Galatians 5:15, Apostle Paul writes "If you bite and devour each other, watch out or you will be destroyed by each other." We must remember that our great enemy is not our spouse, child, co-worker, friend, or neighbor, but the devil. This is why Ephesians 6:12 states emphatically that, "We are not fighting against flesh-and-blood enemies, but against evil rulers and authorities of the unseen world, against mighty powers in this dark world, and against evil spirits in the heavenly places." Our fight is against the devil and his demons.

Third, the devil is constantly on the prowl. The lion is a predator, always looking for and stalking his prey. The devil is like that. Don't be deceived into thinking that "if I don't mess with the devil, he will leave me alone" or be alarmed when the devil shows up or think that somehow, you have done something wrong. I heard someone once say "if you never run into the devil, it means that both of you are going in the same direction." Even when Jesus overcame the devil's temptation in the wilderness, the bible says in Luke 4:13, that the devil left him "for a season" or "until the next opportunity came" or "until an opportune time", meaning that he will be back and at the time or times when you are most vulnerable. So, stay alert.

Fourthly, when the devil is prowling, he is not just taking a walk, he has an evil intent. He is looking for someone to devour. This tells me right away that he cannot devour everyone. So, when he sizes up his prey, he is looking for certain signs and indices that identify that person as someone that he can devour, or he targets an otherwise strong person during a vulnerable time or in an area of vulnerability. If we know what indicators he is looking for, then we can guard against becoming his prey. Below, we discuss some of the ways that we can guard against falling prey to the enemy.

Fifthly, make no mistake, if you give the devil the chance, he will devour you. He does not play nice. His entire ministry on earth is to steal, kill and destroy. He wants to devour you by any means necessary, including sickness, poverty, affliction and ultimately death. If you let him, the devil will kill you. I know well-meaning Christians who have been devoured by the devil, and died an untimely death because they opened the door to the enemy through wrong thinking, wrong speaking, wrong choices, isolation, fear, a lack of knowledge of the word, and so on.

During the time that I was writing this book, the Lord gave me a vision that vividly illustrates how the devil operates. In the vision, I was in a house with family and friends. One of the young adults was playing with a toddler. Little by little, I saw them gravitating away from the other members of the family, towards the door. The toddler would wander off and the young adult would go after her, take her hand and walk with her up and down the hallway leading to the door. They were gradually heading towards the door. I looked straight at the door and saw an animal pacing back and forth in front of the door. At first blush, and from a distance, it looked like a big, brown fluffy cat. But I decided to investigate. As I came close to the door, I was alarmed and said in a concerned voice "It is a lion". Right outside that door, was a fully grown lioness, pacing back and forth, looking as demure and harmless as a cat, but just waiting for the kids to venture outside the protection of the door. I looked again at the door and wondered why I could see through a closed door. Well, the door was shut, but it had huge cracks and places where whole panels of wood were missing. The gaps in the door were big enough for the lioness to have squeezed in, but it didn't, because it had no right to. You see, that door had the blood of the lamb on the doorposts. The blood of Jesus is a hedge of protection around that house and its occupants, and as long as they stayed under that protection, they were safe. The devil could not come in at will. He cannot step over the hedge, but he prowls and waits patiently to see whether he could entice, lure or seduce those kids to venture outside the door, and in so doing, remove the hedge of protection. It's like Ecclesiastes 10:8 (KJV) states, ". . .whoso breaketh an hedge, a serpent shall bite him." The missing panels and chunks of wood in the door were areas where wrong thinking, speaking, actions and beliefs were witling away at the door, and progressively breaking down the protection that it provided. In the vision, I immediately pulled up one of the wood panels, the largest one, that had slid down and latched the door. There were still gaps in the door, but the biggest one was closed. Now the lioness could not come in, even if she tried. I literally shut the door in the devil's face and that is what we should do in our lives and homes.

Here are some of the ways that we can open the door to the devil:

1. **By Knowingly or Unknowingly Giving Him Our Authority:** As Christians, God has given you and me power and authority in the earth. So, whatever the devil does in my life is because I, or someone in authority over me or in relationship with me, authorized him either knowingly or unknowingly. Someone opened the door to the devil in word, thought, or deed.

2. **By Our Spoken Word:** Proverbs 18:21 states that "Death and life are in the power of the tongue." When we speak death or say unbiblical things, we employ the devil. When we speak forth life and the Word of God, we employ angels. Psalm 103:20–21 states: "Praise the Lord, you angels, you mighty ones who carry out his plans, listening for each of his commands (hearkening to the voice of his word). Yes, praise the Lord, you armies of angels who serve him and do his will!"

> *When we speak death or say unbiblical things we employ the devil. When we speak forth life and the word of God, we employ angels.*

Angels are always listening or hearkening for the Word of God. When we give voice to the word, their ears perk up. It is their calling card. Once the Word of God is spoken, the angels, hasten to execute the spoken word. This means that whatever good I want to see in my life, I can authorize it by speaking the word of God. So, in order to take control over my life, I must begin to speak like I created the earth. I am not going to tolerate debt, sickness, oppression and so forth in my life. I am going to change things with the words of my mouth, like God did in creation. When we speak and continue to speak the Word of God, we will shut the door in the face of the devil and transform everything around us to conform to the spoken word.

3. **Making Wrong Choices:** In Romans 6:16 the Bible gives us an insight into one of the devil's key strategies. It states: 'Don't you realize that you become the slave of whatever you choose to obey? You can be a slave to sin, which leads to death, or you can choose to obey God, which leads to righteous living." So many people have become slaves of the devil by making wrong choices. When you choose to sin, you willingly surrender your authority and submit yourself as a slave to the devil.

4. **Unmet Physical Needs:** Unmet physical needs can predispose a person to thinking thoughts, speaking words and making choices that open the door to the devil. Dr. Charles Stanley, senior pastor of First Baptist Church in Atlanta, Georgia, and founder of In Touch Ministries, has developed the acronym HALT to explain this propensity. Dr. Stanley explains, "HALT stands for hungry, angry, lonely and tired – four states in which we will likely make poor choices" (Dr. Charles Stanley, *Making Decisions God's Way*). He continues "Satan never plays fair – he attacks when you are down. Just think of the acronym HALT, and be

on guard whenever you're hungry, angry, lonely or tired" (Stanley).

If you've been or are going through a major trial, temptation or trauma, you are vulnerable and need to be especially careful. Be on your guard!

The good news is that the devil's bag of tricks is limited: in 1 John 2:16, the Bible says: For all that is in the world—the lust of the flesh, the lust of the eyes, and the pride of life—is not of the Father but is of the world.

That's it; all of it. The devil's bag of tricks consists of the lust of the flesh, the lust of the eyes, and the pride of life. This is what he tempted the first Adam with, and this is what he tempted Jesus, the last Adam, with. This is what he tempts us with every day. Jesus overcame, and so can we.

> *In order to take control over my life, I must begin to speak like I created the earth.*

With Authority Comes Responsibility

God has given us authority, and along with that, the responsibility to exercise that authority. What that means is that God will not do for me what he has already done or what he has directed me to do. Let me illustrate. The power company is responsible to supply power to my house. When my house was being constructed, they partnered with the builder to ensure that my house was wired for electricity and that the appropriate equipment was installed to guarantee my access to electric power. However, once the house was built and I moved in, the power company would not come to my house to flip the switch so that I could have light. That was my responsibility. If I did not flip the switch to turn on the light, I could have sat in my house in complete darkness for months, even though my house was fully equipped for and powered by electricity. In Christ, God has provided everything I need to reign in life. Second Peter 1:3 declares that God's divine power has given me all things that pertain to life and godliness through the knowledge of Christ. God has healed me, blessed me, anointed me, empowered me, and supplied my needs. It is already done! But I have to learn how to "flip the switch" to access and deploy all those resources that God has made available to me in Christ.

Some examples will help clarify this point. In James 4:7, God told us to "resist the devil and he will flee from you." It is an utter waste of time for a Christian to wail, bemoan the activities of the devil in his/her life, and pray fervently for God to come, resist, and stop the devil. God will not do it! Why? Because he has deputized us to do it. Jesus has conquered the devil. Our job it to resist him and shut down his operation in our lives.

Same thing with preaching the gospel. In Matthew 28:19–20, Jesus said to us as believers, "Go therefore and make disciples of all the nations, baptizing them in the name of the Father and of the Son and of the Holy Spirit, teaching them to observe all things that I have commanded you; and lo, I am with you always, even to the end of the age." And, in Acts 1:8, Jesus told us to be witnesses for Him and preach the gospel in Judea, Samaria, and to the uttermost parts of the earth. These scriptures make clear that God has delegated to us the work of preaching the gospel and discipling people. In 2 Corinthians 5:11–21, the Bible declares that God has made us His ambassadors, committed into our hands the "ministry of reconciliation," and sent us to reconcile the world back to Him. God will not come to earth to preach to people, nor will he send angels to share the gospel. God's part in the redemption story is done. We now have to do our part. If Christians choose not to reconcile the world to God, then God will do what it takes to get us out of our comfort zones to preach the gospel. For the apostles, it was persecution that got them to break their huddle in Jerusalem and scatter, preaching as they went.

Praying for God to save our loved ones or neighbors without being willing to be used to share the gospel with them is severely flawed. This is why in Acts 10:4–6, when the angel appeared to Cornelius, he did not share the gospel with him. Rather, he asked him to: "Send men to Joppa, and send for Simon whose surname is Peter. He is lodging with Simon, a tanner, whose house is by the sea. He will tell you what you must do."

> *God will not do for me what he has already done or what He has directed me to do.*

Only when Peter came and preached the gospel did the Holy Spirit fall on Cornelius and his household. When we do our part, we activate the finished work of Christ, and the Holy Spirit, God's birthing agent, will draw souls to Jesus.

This also is why some prayers for healing are ineffective. In Matthew 10:8 Jesus told the disciples to "heal the sick," not pray for the sick and ask God to heal them. The distinction is clear. In one situation, the disciple feels helpless and pleads frantically with God to come and heal the sick person. In the other situation, the disciple recognizes that God has already done His part and that the power to heal has been delegated to him/her and so speaks with authority to the sickness to vacate that body. And the sickness will obey as commanded.

PRINCIPLE 3: God Our Father Gave Us the Ability to Create Our World

God our Father created the world with His spoken word. Then he made us in His image and gave us the same creative ability and authority. We can create our world, the same way that God created the earth, by speaking. In Genesis 1:1–3, the Bible says, "In the beginning, God created the heavens and the earth. The earth was without form and empty, and darkness covered the deep waters. And the Spirit of God was hovering over the surface of the waters. Then God said, 'Let there be light,' and there was light."

Note that the earth was without form and empty, and darkness was over the deep until God began to speak. God didn't say what he saw; rather, He declared what he wanted to see, and as he spoke it forth, it came into being. He said, "Let there be light, and there was light." He continued to speak until he transformed everything in sight. He spoke forth order where there was chaos, light in place of darkness, and he filled the empty earth, sky, and seas with living creatures without number. He spoke until what he saw in the natural matched what he wanted to see. Romans 4:17, says that God "calls into existence the things that do not exist." This is precisely what He did in Genesis.

> *Jesus has conquered the devil. Our job is to resist him and shut down his operation in our lives.*

God gave us the same creative power in our mouths to create life or death in our world. Proverbs 18:21 states, "Death and life are in the power of the tongue, and those who love it will eat its fruits." What this scripture is saying, is that my words are containers, filled with life or death. My words can create the future I speak forth, whether good or bad. Second Corinthians 4:13 tells us how this principle operates. It states, "Since we have the same spirit of faith according to what has been written, 'I believed, and so I spoke,' we also believe, and so we also speak."

If we truly believe something in our hearts, and speak it forth with our mouths, it will come to pass. In Mark 11:23, Jesus outlined this principle. He said, "Truly I tell you, whoever says to this mountain, 'Go, throw yourself into the sea,' and does not doubt in his heart but believes that what he says will happen, he will have whatever he says."

The principle is clear, my words are powerful! If my words are powerful, imagine, how much more powerful are the words of God. The Bible says of God's Word:

> *Every word I speak is on assignment.*

> For as the rain and the snow come down from heaven and do not return there but water the earth, making it bring forth and sprout, giving seed to the sower and bread to the eater, so shall my word be that goes out from my mouth; it shall not return to me empty, but it shall accomplish that which I purpose, and shall succeed in the thing for which I sent it.

Simply stated, the word of God coming out of my mouth, in faith, is the most potent weapon known to man. What this means, is that every word I speak is on assignment. Once I believe the Word in my heart and launch it forth via the spoken word, it will not return empty; it will achieve its creative purpose and assignment. It is unstoppable!

This is exactly how we became children of God. Romans 10:9, states: "The word is near you, in your mouth and in your heart" (that is, the word of faith that we proclaim); because, if you confess with your mouth that Jesus is Lord and believe in your heart that God raised him from the dead, you will be saved." We believed the gospel in our hearts and confessed our faith with our mouths, and we were saved! In Colossians 2:6, the Bible states, "As you have therefore received Christ Jesus the Lord, so walk in Him." How did we receive Christ? We believed in our hearts and we confessed with our mouths. Well, that is also how to "walk in Him", meaning, live the Christian life and accomplish the purposes of God. Believe in the heart and speak forth with the mouth. What you say shall come to pass.

This kingdom principle will work for anyone who applies it. In Luke 8:43–44, the Bible reports how a nameless woman applied this principle to schedule her miracle while Jesus was on His way to the home of Jairus.

> *My words are containers, filled with life or death. My words can create the future I speak forth, whether good or bad.*

As Jesus went with him, he was surrounded by the crowds. A woman in the crowd had suffered for twelve years with constant bleeding, and she could find no cure. Coming up behind Jesus, she touched the fringe of his robe. Immediately, the bleeding stopped. "Who touched me?" Jesus asked. Everyone denied it, and Peter said, "Master, this whole crowd is pressing up against you." But Jesus said, "Someone deliberately touched me, for I felt healing power go out from me."

Even though Jesus was thronged by a large crowd, one woman deliberately drew healing power from Him without His express consent. How did she do it?

> *What I believe and say about myself has the greatest impact on my life more than any other person's words spoken over me.*

Matthew's account of the same incident gives us some insight. In Matthew 9:21 (AMP), the Bible says of the woman, "For she had been saying to herself, "If I only touch His outer robe, I will be healed." We do not know how long this woman loaded and launched those faith-filled words. But, again and again, she kept saying to herself, "If I only touch His outer robe, I will be healed." Well, she did, and she was. This woman initiated, scheduled, and activated her miracle by her faith-filled words. She believed in her heart, declared it with her mouth, and acted upon what she believed. Jesus said to her, "Daughter, be encouraged! Your faith has made you well." And she was healed at that moment.

Several years ago, I applied this principle to banish sickness from my life. Before then, every fall and winter, I would catch a cold, several colds, and sometimes the flu. I had heard, over the years, that fall and winter is the "flu season," and I believed it. Sure enough, every fall and winter, I would get the cold and sometimes the flu. One day, while listening to Andrew Wommack, it dawned on me that the cold and flu are not provided under the new covenant. They were in my life only because I had allowed them to be. So, I purposed, that day, that I would not have the cold or flu anymore. Since then, every year, I declare in faith, "It is *not* cold or flu season at my house. I oppose sickness in all its forms. I declare that the blood of Jesus is on patrol 24/7 in my life, enforcing the covenant of life and health that I have in Christ. I have the life of God in me. The blood of Jesus is speaking abundant life to every cell, tissue, and organ of my body. The blood is speaking over me and my family—victory, increase, favor, divine protection, peace, abundance, divine health, and promotion." Since then, I have never had the flu or cold ever again. I simply disallowed it in my house and life! And the cold and flu obeyed my words and stayed away from me.

On another occasion, I used the same principle to keep a bird from building a nest in my dryer vent. We had tried everything we could to stop that bird, all to no avail. We closed off the dryer vent, but the bird pecked until it removed, broke down, or broke through the protective barrier and resumed building its nest. Eventually, it hatched five little birds in our dryer vent. We relocated the babies, but the mother persisted in returning to the dryer vent. Finally, in desperation, I asked the Lord what to do. And He said, "Speak to the bird." And I did! I spoke to the bird, denied it access to my house, and disallowed it from coming to my home anymore. I declared to the bird, that it will *not* build a nest in my dryer vent.

Since that day to today, that bird never again came into my dryer vent. The Word of God spoken in faith terminated its access and redirected it away from my home.

> *The word of God coming out of my mouth, in faith, is the most powerful weapon known to man.*

Principle 4: My Sonship is My Key to the Supernatural

Just like an Asian man will reproduce an Asian child and an African America man will reproduce an African American child, God is a spirit and brings forth spiritual children. When we receive Christ, our spirit is born again. We are born of the spirit of God, and instantly we are a new creation in the spirit. In our spirits, we look perfect, just like Christ. Explaining this to Nicodemus, Jesus said in John

3:6, "That which is born of the flesh is flesh and that which is born of the spirit is spirit." Under the new covenant, everything that God has and gives to us is already provided and made available in the spirit. When we are born again, God's provision for our health, wellbeing, finances, and so forth are all complete and all provided in the spirit. All I need to do is to renew my mind and release my faith to appropriate the provisions that God has already made available to me in the spirit and bring them into physical manifestation.

However, functionally, most people do not acknowledge the spirit realm. The problem is, God is a spirit. I cannot contact God using my body; five senses; or my mind, will, and emotions. John 4:24 makes

> *To be in relationship with God, commune with God, or access the resources of God, I must engage the spiritual dimension.*

this point. God is a spirit, and the way to contact Him is in/through the spirit. So, to be in relationship with God, commune with God, or access the resources of God, I must be aware of and engage the spiritual dimension.

First Corinthians 2:9–13 states:

> But as it is written: "Eye has not seen, nor ear heard, nor have entered into the heart of man, the things which God has prepared for those who love Him." But God has revealed *them* to us through His Spirit. For the Spirit searches all things, yes, the deep things of God. For what man knows the things of a man except the spirit of the man which is in him? Even so no one knows the things of God except the Spirit of God. Now we have received, not the spirit of the world, but the Spirit who is from God, that we might know the things that have been freely given to us by God. These things we

also speak, not in words which man's wisdom teaches but which the Holy Spirit teaches, comparing spiritual things with spiritual.

> *If you want to know and access the things God has for you, you must learn to "speak spirit".*

This scripture makes it abundantly clear that God our Father has provided lavishly and fabulously for our wellbeing. All these provisions are located in the spirit, and he has given us the Holy Spirit as our friend and partner to help us navigate the spirit realm so that we can know and access the things He has freely prepared and made ready to us. He states clearly that the natural man, meaning the man operating by his five senses, cannot know or receive the things of God because they are spiritually discerned. It says that the Holy Spirit searches the deep things of God, and he alone knows the mind of God and knows the things freely given to us by God. Further, the scripture says that these things cannot be explained with human wisdom, but only with words "which the Holy Spirit teaches." Translation: If we want to know and access the things God has for us, we must learn to "speak spirit."

To "speak spirit" means, firstly, speaking the word of God. In John 6:63, Jesus said, "And the very words I have spoken to you are spirit and life". When we speak the word of God, we are speaking words "which the Holy Spirit teaches" and bringing the life of God into the situation. The word of God is spirit, so, when we proclaim the word of God, we cut through every obstruction, barrier or hindrance in the spirit realm and gain direct access to the resources God has provided for us. Secondly, to "speak spirit" means, speaking in tongues. Acts 2:4 explains: "And everyone present was filled with the Holy Spirit and began speaking in other languages, or in other tongues, as the Holy Spirit gave them this ability." So, speaking in tongues is speaking the language of the Holy Spirit. Again, it cuts through every impediment or barrier and nothing is lost in the translation. When we speak or pray in tongues, we are talking, spirit to spirit.

> *When I pray in tongues, the Holy Spirit "docks" me into the throne room of God.*

This is why speaking in tongues is so critical to success in the Christian walk! The way that I think about it is this: for over two decades, I have worked in corporate America. My job involved a lot of business travel. Many times, when I was outside the office, security patches, software, and other updates were installed. When I got back to the office and docked my laptop in the docking station, immediately the laptop goes to work, identifying all the patches and updates intended for me and begins to download them and apply them to my computer. So, if I did not dock into the office over a long period of time, this could affect my ability to do my job as I would not have access to the software and other updates provided by my employer. Ultimately, I could lose connectivity and be cut off from the company network.

This is what the Holy Spirit does. When I pray in tongues, the Holy Spirit "docks" me into the throne room of God. He then goes to work, searching the deep things of God, identifying the plan, modifications, provisions, and updates from the throne room of God for me. He identifies all the things, people and resources that God has provided, prepared and made ready to meet my needs. Then He downloads them into my

> *My ability to walk with, listen to, and obey the Holy Spirit is critical to accessing all the abundance that God has provided for me.*

spirit. Sometimes, he deposits them in my "heart" and I "know" them, not because someone told me, but because I have a "knowing" from the Holy Spirit. In these types of situations, you often can't explain how you know, you just do. At other times, He deposits them in my heart or my imagination and enables me to "see" them, not with my physical eyes, but with the eyes of my heart. This ministry of the Holy Spirit has been such a tremendous blessing to me and has gotten me out of so many tough situations!

Several years ago, I went to an office to obtain a very important legal document. I needed this document by a deadline that was a couple months away. But, up until then, I had thought nothing of it. It shouldn't be a problem, I thought to myself. I was qualified and eligible to receive this document. All I needed to do was to arrange time off from work, so I could go to the appropriate government office and obtain the document. On the day when I go there, there was a long line. After standing in line for over thirty minutes, I got up to the service window and the staff informed me that the law had changed and I was no longer eligible to receive the document. This was a major blow! I had to get this document before the deadline or I could face serious consequences. Now, I was really in trouble. I turned to the Holy Spirit! I fasted and prayed in tongues over the situation. I knew that God had provided this document for me, but I didn't know how to access it. Then in prayer, the Holy Spirit showed me the face of a man. This was the man who had been commissioned by the Lord to give me the document. So, the next week, I went back to the office, but when I visually scanned the service windows, the man wasn't there. I stood in line, but once again, when I got to the service window, I was told by the staff that the laws had changed and I no longer qualified to receive this critical document. This happened three more times. All this while, I continued to pray. The situation was getting desperate, as the deadline was now only a few weeks away. Each time, when I went to the office, I would visually scan the service windows and look at the faces of the employees working that day. Each of those times, I did not see the man whom the Lord had shown me in prayer. So, I would stand in line, and when it was my turn, I would go up to the next available agent, and inevitably, I would be told the same thing – the laws have changed and we can't give you this document. Well, I refused to give up, because the Holy Spirit had shown me that the Lord had provided this document for me and instructed a specific man to give it to me. On the fifth trip, as I got into the waiting area and looked at the service windows, lo and behold, the man that I had seen in prayer, was sitting at one of the service windows! My heart jumped for joy! I knew today was my day! I stood in line, but I was determined not to go to any other window, but his window. I knew the Lord had instructed him to give me the document. I stood in line and prayed! When my turn came, he was attending to another person, so I asked the person behind me in line to go ahead of me. I was not going to any other window today, but that man's window. When his window opened up, I went forward and made my request for the document. He looked at me and said "the law has changed and you are no longer eligible to receive this document, *but I will give it to you*, and he proceeded to do just that. When I left that office and got to the parking lot, I jumped up and shouted praises to the Lord, blessing the God of heaven, whose faithfulness is for ever and ever. I would never have been able to overcome the changed law without the ministry of the Holy Spirit, showing me the man that God has prepared, instructed and made ready to issue the document I needed. God had provided this document for me, but I would never have accessed this provision of God, without the help of the Holy Spirit.

This experience illustrates a key point. My ability to engage, walk with, listen to, and obey the Holy Spirit is critical to accessing all the abundance that has been freely given to me by God. This is why Romans 8:14 states, "As many as are led by the spirit of God, they are the sons of God." Understanding and walking in the rights and privileges of sonship require me to stay connected to God through the Holy Spirit.

Sonship means knowing and exercising my spiritual authority. It both requires and enables me to be aware of and engage with God in the spirit. Sonship is my portal to accessing the supernatural and all the provisions that God has prepared and kept ready for me in the spirit.

PRINCIPLE 5: "Sons" Have Manifestations

The Bible declares in Romans 8:19 (KJV) that all of creation is waiting for the manifestation of the "sons" of God. These are men and women who apply the sonship principles and walk in the pattern of sonship, to liberate themselves and others from sickness, poverty, fear, oppression, bondage, sin, failure, defeat and so on. They demonstrate by their obedience and example that the principles and pattern are as effective today as they were when Jesus walked the earth!

Here is the point. Mature sons and daughters of God exercise and manifest the power of God to liberate creation, including themselves and others, from bondage! Jesus repeatedly illustrated this principle. He exercised power over all creation. In John 1: 38–44, he raised the dead; in Matthew 8:26–27, he calmed the sea and walked on water. In John 2:3–17 and Matthew 17:24–27, He exercised power over nations, institutions, finances, and the economy. And Acts 10:38 records that He demonstrated absolute power over natural laws by performing miracles, signs, and wonders. Jesus is the pattern.

Regarding sons and daughters of God, Mark 16:15 declares: "these signs shall accompany those who have believed. In my name, they will cast out demons, they will speak with new tongues, they will pick up serpents and if they drink any deadly poison it will not hurt them, they will lay hands on the sick and they shall recover."

In John 14:12, Jesus said, "I tell you the truth, anyone who believes in me will do the same works I have done, and even greater works, because I am going to be with the Father."

He backed up this declaration with a grant of power. In Luke 10:19, he states: "Behold, I give you the authority to trample on serpents and scorpions, and over all the power of the enemy, and nothing shall by any means hurt you."

This means that we are duly deputized to stop, frisk, arrest, sentence and execute God's judgement on the devil and all his agents, including demons, all types of physical, mental and emotional sickness and so on.

The apostles walked in this pattern. Regarding Apostle Peter, in Acts of the Apostles 5:15–16, the Bible records that: "As a result of the apostles' work, sick people were brought out into the streets on beds and mats so that Peter's

> *We are duly deputized to stop, frisk, arrest, sentence and execute God's judgement on the devil and his agents.*

shadow might fall across some of them as he went by. Crowds came from the villages around Jerusalem, bringing their sick and those possessed by evil spirits, and they were all healed."

For Apostle Paul, Acts of the Apostles 19:11–12 states that: "God gave Paul the power to perform unusual miracles. When handkerchiefs or aprons that had merely touched his skin were placed on sick people, they were healed of their diseases, and evil spirits were expelled."

"Who are you?" is a question about sonship mandate and manifestation.

The Devil Knows the Sonship Pattern

The devil knows men and women who are walking in the sonship pattern. Acts 19:13, tells the story of a group of Jews who were traveling from town to town, casting out evil spirits. They tried to use the name of the Lord Jesus in their incantation, saying:

> I command you in the name of Jesus, whom Paul preaches, to come out!" Seven sons of Sceva, a Jewish chief priest, were among the exorcists. But one time when they tried to use the name of Jesus to cast out demons, the evil spirit replied, "I know Jesus, and I know Paul, but who are you?" Then the man with the evil spirit leaped on them, overpowered them, and attacked them with such violence that they fled from the house, naked and battered.

The seven sons of Sceva were either not in Christ or did not know who they were in Christ. No wonder the evil spirit did not know who they were either. Note that they were sons of a "Jewish chief priest," meaning that they had religious standing and pedigree. Also, they obviously knew about Jesus and Paul and must have either heard about or witnessed the power in the name of Jesus to cast out devils. So, they knew that evil spirits obey commands issued in the name of Jesus, and they expected the same results. What they did not know was that religious pedigree and knowing about Jesus was not enough. It matters who is using the name and whether or not they are in relationship with Christ. It matters whether they have Jesus's authorization or power of attorney to use His name. It matter's whether they had been deputized by Christ. They didn't know that, but the devil knew and was royally ticked off by their aggravation when they could not answer the simple question, who are you?

Who are you? That is a question that we must all be prepared to answer. It is a question about sonship mandate and manifestation. It is a question that says in essence, show me your sonship credentials. The whole of creation is waiting for "sons" of God to manifest; that includes the devil. When you begin to manifest the sonship principles, the devil will try to intimidate, deceive, or steal your confidence. He does not want you to manifest as a son or daughter of God. He wants to keep you and all creation in bondage. This is why it is mission critical that you must know, from the Scriptures, who you are in Christ, and that your identity is strongly rooted, not in your performance, your good works, your pedigree, or anything else, but in Christ alone!

Also, when you choose to manifest as a "son" of God, the devil will challenge your sonship, the same way he challenged Jesus. In Matthew 4:3, he said to Jesus, "If you are the son of God, tell these stones to become loaves of bread." Keep in mind that this was right after Jesus had been publicly declared to be the Son of God by the Father. In Matthew 3:16–17, the Bible states: "After his baptism, as

Jesus came up out of the water, the heavens were opened and he saw the Spirit of God descending like a dove and settling on him. And a voice from heaven said, 'This is my dearly loved Son, who brings me great joy.'"

This is the one time in Scripture when the entire Godhead—the Father, the Son, and the Holy Spirit congregated in the earth, in one place, at one time, for one single purpose, to publicly confirm and affirm the identity and sonship of Christ. But that did not stop the devil! Right after that, he challenged Jesus's sonship. But Jesus knew who He was and quickly put the devil in his place. Wielding the sword of the Spirit, He said, "No! The Scriptures say, say, people do not live by bread alone, but by every word that comes from the mouth of God" (Matthew 4:4). Jesus did not make this about Himself, who He was, what He has, or who He knows. He made it all about God and His Word. He did not need to prove Himself to the devil, nor did He need to show off in pride. He is the Son of God. He knew that and walked in that authority without a flinch.

This is where the first Adam, and his wife, Eve, failed. Luke 3:38 tells us that Adam was "the son of God. But, sure enough, the devil challenged his sonship and that of his wife Eve. In Genesis 3:4, when Eve told the devil about God's direction not to eat the fruit from the tree of the knowledge of good and evil, he said to her, "You won't die! God knows that your eyes will be opened as soon as you eat it, and you will be like God." Adam and Eve were already like God. They were made in His image! They were "sons" of God! But, they didn't know their identity or exercise their authority to shut down the devil. So, when he asked them in essence, "Who are you?" they had no valid response. He played to their pride, and they fell for his trick. As a result, they were deceived into disobeying God, and in so doing, lost their authority to the devil.

Who are you? It's not only the devil and his demons who want to know. Your circumstances, giants, mountains, and emotions will ask you that same question. Sickness will ask you that question. Relationship problems will ask you that question. Failure and poverty will ask you that question. Success will also ask you that question. The devil challenged Jesus's sonship, right after a high point in His ministry, the glorious public declaration and open display by the Godhead confirming Him as the Son of God. The devil showed up right after that to ask Him essentially, "Who are you?" If he did it to Jesus and to the Adam and Eve, he will do it to us. So, be on your guard.

How you respond to this question is vital. if you don't know your God or who you are in Him, you will have an identity crisis and lose your way like Adam and Eve did. I heard Creflo Dollar once say, that "a behavior problem is an identity problem." It certainly was for Adam and Eve. The same thing applies today. A young girl who does not know who she is, or whose she is, is more likely to fall prey to the enchantment of the enemy or the antics of a devious young man wanting to lead her astray. A young man who does not know who he is, is more likely to join a gang to "belong" and gain a sense of identity and self-worth.

God's plan is for "sons" of God to walk in the same authority today that Jesus demonstrated in Matthew 4. To do that, we must know not only who we are, but whose we are. Do you know who you are? If you do, then you can stand your ground and instruct the devil and his principalities and powers of their defeat and your victory in Christ. You can tell them about Colossians 2:13–15 which testifies that "God made us alive with Christ, for he forgave all our sins. He canceled the record of the charges against us and took it away by nailing it to the cross. In this way, he disarmed the spiritual rulers and authorities. He shamed them publicly by his victory over them on the cross." If you know who you are in Christ, you can be strong in the Lord, and in the power of His might, put on the whole armor of God, stand against the wiles of the devil, wrestle him and his demons to the ground, withstand them and having done all, to keep standing (Ephesians 6:10–18). Daniel 11:32 puts it succinctly: "the people that do know their God, *shall* be strong and do exploits."

PRINCIPLE 6: "Sons" of God Refuse to Settle for Less Than God's Best

Mature sons and daughters of God refuse to settle for less that their inheritance. They refuse to settle for the status quo or to fit into the categories defined by people, when those parameters do not line up with the word of God. Sons and daughters of God refuse to settle for a life of sin or bondage when they know that they were made for much more. They find out what the will of their father is, and they go for it with gusto, even when it means coloring outside the lines set by convention, culture or their limited resources. Walking as a son or daughter of God requires boldness, courage and honesty. Boldness to face the giants without, courage to confront the enemy within, and honesty to speak the truth to oneself, others and God.

Sons and daughters of God refuse to settle for a life that is beneath their inheritance, no matter how long and tedious the struggle. This principle is based on the premise that you cannot change what you tolerate. It is a principle that requires strong personal discipline and a great view of God. Mature sons and daughters of God believe that God is who He says that He is, and that He would do exactly what He says that He would do. So, they don't negotiate, compromise or settle with the devil, their flesh, or their circumstances. They stand resolute on the word of God, even if they stand alone. They refuse to make room for, accommodate or cohabit with sickness, sin, failure, bondage, defeat and anything else that is beneath who they are in Christ.

For "sons" of God, "no" is a complete sentence. They say no to the devil, to sickness, sin, temptation, affliction, bondage, lack and limitations. They say no to anything that opposes the word of God or does not bring glory to God. "Sons" of God do not trifle with sin. They are committed to honoring God and would not want to live a life that would give the enemies of God cause to blaspheme His name. They have an audience of one — God. They know that, even if nobody else knows, God knows, and their sin is a grave dishonor to His Holy name.

> For "sons" of God, "no" is a complete sentence.

Sons and daughters of God live their lives based on biblical convictions. These convictions, formed early in their Christian walk, become the guard rails of their entire lives and help them stay on course. So, when confronted with temptation, sin and compromise, its relatively easy to say no, because their decision was already made, a long time ago. Genesis 39:9, tells of the noble words of Joseph to Potiphar's wife, when she tried, again and again to seduce him. He said: "How could I do such a wicked thing? It would be a great sin against God."

Not only do "sons" of God refuse to settle for sin and compromise, they also do not settle for the status quo or the convenient. They want everything that God has provided and made available for them. Simply stated, they want their inheritance in God and they are willing to fight for it. Three of my favorite stories in the Bible illustrate this point.

Numbers 27 records the story of five radical women, Mahlah, Noah, Hoglah, Milcah and Tirzah, the daughters of Zelophehad, who confronted and overcame entrenched laws to obtain their inheritance. In the culture of Israel at that time, women did not inherit land. Land was family property and passed solely by male descent, to ensure that it stays within the tribe. But these women would not stand for the status quo. They came to Moses and said:

> "Our father died in the wilderness," "But he had no sons. Why should the name of our father disappear from his clan just because he had no sons? Give us property along with the rest of our relatives" (Numbers 27:3-4).

This was unheard of! In a society where women were to be seen and not heard, making a request like this required great courage and boldness. It required guts!

> *"Sons" of God want their inheritance in God and they are willing to fight for it.*

But remember, you cannot change what you tolerate. These women would not settle for the status quo that denied them their father's inheritance because they were female. So, they went to Moses and asked for their inheritance. Their request was so novel that Moses did not have an answer. This was a case of first impression. No one had ever made such a request before. So, Moses took their petition to the Lord.

If I were to ask a hundred people what they thought God's answer would be, most people would think that God would say no, or maybe even rebuke the women for their impudence. But that was not the case. "The Lord replied to Moses, "The claim of the daughters of Zelophehad is legitimate. You must give them a grant of land along with their father's relatives. Assign them the property that would have been given to their father" (Numbers 27:7). Then the Lord went even further! He said to Moses "And give the following instructions to the people of Israel: If a man dies and has no son, then give his inheritances to his daughters" (Numbers 27:8).

Wow! Not only did these radical daughters of God receive their inheritance, they changed the law in Israel! In Joshua 17:3-6, when the Israelites entered the promised land, they again made their request to Joshua and received their grant of land. The Bible records that, "As a result, Manasseh's total allocation came to ten parcels of land, ...because the female descendants of Manasseh received a grant of land along with the male descendants" (Joshua 17:5-6). These women changed the destiny of their tribe!

1 Samuel 1, tells of the story of Hannah, a woman who simply would not settle for barrenness, even though she was dearly loved by her husband. She would not settle for the status quo. For Hannah, the choice portion of meat she got from her husband was not enough. She wanted more! 1 Samuel 1:10 states: "Hannah was in deep anguish, crying bitterly as she prayed to the Lord. And she made this vow: "O Lord of Heaven's armies, if you will look upon my sorrow and answer my prayer and give me a son, then I will give him back to you. He will be yours for his entire lifetime."

> *"Sons" of God live their lives based on biblical convictions.*

The way I imagine that this happened, was that God was walking the courts of heaven, listening to Hannah's tearful petition. Then she made that vow, and the Lord stopped in His tracks. "What did she just say?" He asked? And the angels repeated Hannah's petition and her bold vow. And the Lord beamed with joy and said "It's a deal!" This was a daughter of God coming confidently to her father with a bold request. God answered her prayer.

Because of her refusal to settle for the status quo, Hannah not only gave birth to several children, but she brought forth Samuel, who was by all accounts, the greatest priest in Israel. He has two books that bear his name in the bible, and he anointed king David, the greatest king of Israel. The amazing thing is that their family is not even from the tribe of Levi, the priestly tribe in Israel. This one woman, by her refusal to settle for "her lot in life" executed a shift and qualified her womb to bring forth a son, who was both a priest and prophet, and who changed the destiny of the nation of Israel.

The same thing with Blind Bartimaeus. He would not settle for the status quo. He was blind, but he wanted out and he was willing to fight for it. Remember, you cannot change what you tolerate. Jesus had just left Jericho, with a large crowd in tow. Bartimaeus was a blind beggar sitting beside the road. When he "heard that Jesus of Nazareth was nearby, he began to shout, "Jesus, Son of David, have mercy on me!" "Be quiet!" many of the people yelled at him. But he only shouted louder, "Son of David, have mercy on me!" When Jesus heard him, he stopped and said, "Tell him to come here." Bartimaeus threw aside his coat, jumped up and came to Jesus. Jesus asked him "What do you want me to do for you?" "My Rabbi", the blind man said, "I want to see!" And Jesus said to him, "Go for your faith has healed you." And he was healed instantly (Mark 10:46-52).

Bartimaeus would not settle for being blind. He would not be stopped by convention, protocol or the disapproval of other people.

He was loud and insistent. He threw aside his beggar's coat and jumped up over the objection of people. His persistence got the attention of Jesus. The funny thing is, as soon as Jesus called him to come, the same crowd that had tried to silence him and told him to "be quiet" earlier, now said to him "Cheer up, come on, he's calling you." People are fickle! Do not let the fear of people —what they will think, say or do, stop you from going for God's best!

The common thread in these bible accounts are individuals who wanted more! They believed that God could do more and they had the temerity to ask Him to do it for them, and He did! They did not let convention, existing laws, public shame or ridicule keep them from God's best. They wanted more!

> Sons and daughters of God have to be willing to say to God, "Father, I want some more."

Growing up, I was a voracious reader. I loved to read and enjoyed the works of Mark Twain, Charles Dickens, Shakespeare, Jonathan Swift, and fairy tales like Rapunzel, Rumpelstiltskin, Little Red Riding Hood and so on. One of the books that made a lasting impression on me was "Oliver Twist" by Charles Dickens. This is a story about a poor orphan boy who was in an English workhouse, where he was overworked and underfed. His diet consisted of a daily scoop of gruel, a thin liquid food of oatmeal boiled in water or milk. One day, out of sheer desperation, he mustered up enough courage to go up to Mr. Bumble, the master of the work house and say in a faltering voice, "Please sir, I want some more." Those words were the undoing of Oliver Twist! The master and others in charge of the workhouse were aghast with shock. And the refrain "Oliver has asked for more" reverberated around the work house as it was repeated by one person after the other in utter disbelief. The shock was palpable and they declared with finality "That boy will be hung!" Mr. Bumble intoned, "I never was more convinced of anything in my life, than I am that that boy will come to be hung" (Charles Dickens, *Oliver Twist*). Oliver was beaten, held in solitary confinement in a dark room, and the next day, a bill was posted offering a reward of five pounds to anyone who would take him off the hands of the parish, for his profane offense of asking for more gruel.

> *Do not let the fear of people — what they will think, say or do, stop you from going for God's best!*

Sadly, some people think of God like that cruel work master. They think that He wants to give us the most meager of provisions and would whack us on the head if we dared to ask for more. But, that is not the God of heaven. He is a great God, and a good, good Father. He is a rich God, and he loves lavishly and gives super abundantly. It honors Him when we ask Him for more. It shows that we have faith in Him and trust in His love for us. Sons and daughters of God have to be willing to say to God, "Father, I want some more" – more of God, more of His word, more of His favor, presence, healing, provision, victory, power, and so on. Ephesians 3:20 (AMP) states, that God is "able to carry out His purpose and do superabundantly more than all that we dare ask or think, infinitely beyond our greatest prayers, hopes or dreams, according to His power that is at work within us." This is why He invites us to ask boldly and assures us in Matthew 7:8 that "For everyone who asks, receives. Everyone who seeks, finds. And to everyone who knocks, the door will be opened."

PRINCIPLE 7: God Will Not Release Authority and Dominion into the Hands of Children

Just like you will not give your five-year-old the keys to drive your car, God will not release inheritance and the associated authority and dominion into the hands of children. Any child of God who wants to obtain his or her inheritance must grow into sonship The Bible describes this growth process and the midwife in the journey to spiritual maturation. Galatians 4:1–3 states:

> Now I say that the heir, as long as he is a child, does not differ at all from a slave, though he is master of all, but is under guardians and stewards until the time appointed by the father. Even so we, when we were children, were in bondage under the elements of the world.

This scripture makes clear that there is a process to grow from childhood to sonship. The Bible says in Romans 8:17 that we are heirs of God and joint heirs with Christ. However, as long as we remain children, there will be no realistic distinction between the outcomes that we experience and that of a slave. We will have all the limitations, lack of power, and helplessness of a slave. But when we invest in growth and maturity, with the Holy Spirit as our birthing agent, we can walk in the authority of sonship. Every child of God has the potential and destiny to become

> *Walking in the sonship pattern is a daily choice. It takes growth, discipline, and refusing to be led by your feelings.*

a mature son or daughter of God. We have all we need to operate as "sons" of God in the earth, but choosing to walk in the sonship pattern is a daily choice. It takes growth, discipline, and refusing to be led by our feelings. Keep in mind that sonship is not a chronological fact. You are not a "son" of God because you have been a Christian for a set number of years. Sonship is a manifestation of growth in the soul—mind, will, and emotions. Neither is sonship a biological fact. New covenant sonship as outlined in Romans 8:14 is gender neutral.

Sonship is a choice. Isaiah 9:6 tells us that a child is born, but a son is given. It states: "For unto us a Child is born, unto us a Son is given; And the government will be upon His shoulder. And His name will be called Wonderful, Counselor, Mighty God, Everlasting Father, Prince of Peace." Whether or not we exercise the rights of sonship depends on our willingness to take on the responsibility. Isaiah 9:6 specifies that how you'll identify the son is that "the government shall be on his shoulder." "Sons" of God are willing to shoulder responsibility and accountability. They are willing to administer the kingdom.

> *"Sons" of God are willing to shoulder responsibility and accountability.*

You and I have a choice in every situation we face, to act as a mature son or daughter, or as a child. Sonship takes faith and requires obedience to the Holy Spirit. A good indicator of whether or not you are a mature son or daughter is in your mind—how you think and what voice you follow. If you are ruled by your emotions, you are a child. If you cater to your flesh, you are a child. If you are led by your five senses, you are a child. If you know what is right to do but choose to act based on how you feel, you are a child. Romans 8:6–8 explains:

> So letting your sinful nature control your mind leads to death. But letting the Spirit control your mind leads to life and peace. For the sinful nature is always

hostile to God. It never did obey God's laws, and it never will. That's why those who are still under the control of their sinful nature can never please God.

The good news is, it doesn't matter how low a son has sunk. Any day he realizes and "comes to himself," he can step right back into sonship. In Luke 15:17, when the prodigal son finally came to himself or came to his senses, he said. "I will arise and go to my father, and will say to him, 'Father, I have sinned against heaven and before you, and I am no longer worthy to be called your son. Make me like one of your hired servants.'"

> *It doesn't matter how low a son has sunk. Any day he realizes and "comes to himself," he can step right back into sonship.*

This was a sonship moment! He had been living like a child: sinful, self-centered, self-willed, irresponsible, independent, and separated from the Father until he came to himself. First, he began to think differently. He saw himself and his situation as the Father sees it. Then he made a decision. He said, I will arise and go to my father—and he did! He acted on his decision to honor and obey his father. This is what "sons" do. They make decisions based on the Word of God, and they follow through! Romans 8:14 states: As many as are led by the Spirit of God, these are the sons of God." Growth into sonship is measurable, not by how much of the Bible you have memorized, how many committees you lead in the church, and so forth. The measure of spiritual maturity and sonship is whose voice you obey. Is it the voice of your flesh, the devil, sin, the world or the voice of the Father?

How to Transition from Childhood into Sonship

1. **Learn Doctrine:** Sons and daughters of God must know the word and ways of God. They must apply themselves, and invest time to grow, learn God's character and how to correctly handle the word of God (2 Timothy 2:15). As Hebrews 6:1–3 admonishes: "So let us stop going over the basic teachings about Christ again and again. Let us go on instead and become mature in our understanding."

2. **Eat Strong Meat:** "Sons" of God are not wimps. Eating strong meat means that you stop being a baby, but rather grow up, train yourself to distinguish between right and wrong, and then train others. Hebrews 5:11-14 rebukes believers who have been believers for so long that they ought to be teaching others. Instead, they are still babies, needing to be fed milk and not solid food. Mature sons and daughters of God must be willing to endure hardness as good soldiers (2 Timothy 2:3). They must commit to serve their Father and His family, the church. Sons and daughters of God invest themselves and their resources to build the kingdom of God.

3. **Be Led by the Spirit:** Sons and daughters of God treasure their relationship with God. They tune in to hear His voice and are led by the Spirit. They say yes to God. In Galatians 5:16, apostle Paul exhorts: "So I say, let the Holy Spirit guide your lives. Then you won't be doing what your sinful nature craves. The sinful nature wants to do evil, which is just the opposite of what the Spirit wants." Spiritual maturity means routinely saying "no" to the sinful nature and "yes" to the Spirit.

4. **Understand the Things Freely Given to us by God:** Mature sons and daughters of God must know their inheritance, so they can administer the estate of their Father to accomplish and execute His will. They must study the Bible to know the provisions of His will, so they can establish it in the earth. Their prayer is, "Your Kingdom come, your will be done on earth, as it is in heaven" (Matthew 6:10). They diligently search the scriptures and seek God in prayer, like Jesus did. They actively engage with the Holy Spirit and pray in the spirit, to know the things "freely given to us by God" (1 Corinthians 2:9–13). This knowledge empowers them to fulfill God's plan and purpose in the earth.

5. **Give up Childish Ways:** A key requirement for sonship is to grow up into spiritual maturity. First Corinthians 13:11 states: "When I was a child, I spoke and thought and reasoned as a child. But when I grew up, I put away childish things." The problem is that many Christians want to walk in the authority and rights of sonship, but they also want to be able to talk, think, and reason like a child at the same time. It does not work that way. Like Joyce Meyer says, "You can be pitiful or powerful, but you can't be both." You cannot complain about every situation, curse people out, gossip, and think anything that comes into your mind for as long as you want about yourself, others, and God and still walk in the authority and rights of sonship. You have to make a choice daily—child or son?

> *The struggle with sin is not evidence of failure; rather, it is evidence of the life of God within and the tenacious work of the Holy Spirit.*

6. **Overcome Sin:** "Sons" of God must reject and oppose sin in all its forms in themselves and others. They are led by the Spirit and learn through training and discipline to say "no" to their sinful nature, desires, and appetites. Sons and daughters of God consecrate themselves to God. When faced with temptation, their motto is "Others may, but I cannot." They make a personal commitment to live lives that bring honor and glory to God, and they follow through. In Romans 8:5–8, apostle Paul explains that the key to overcoming sin is to ensure that we are "controlled by the Holy Spirit", so that we "think about things that please the Spirit." He warns that "the sinful nature is always hostile to God. It never did obey God's laws, and it never will."

So, for the son and daughter of God, the struggle with sin is not evidence of failure; rather, it is evidence of the life of God within and the tenacious work of the Holy Spirit to conform us to the image of Christ. "Sons" of God must commit to this sanctification process.

> "Sons" and daughters of God must be willing to say "Others may, but I cannot."

7. **Be Willing to Partake in the Fellowship of His Suffering:** Jesus suffered, even though he was sinless. Hebrews 4:15 states: "We do not have a high priest who is unable to sympathize with our weaknesses, but one who in every respect was tempted as we are, yet without sin." Then Hebrews 5:8–9, explains: "Even though Jesus was God's son, he learned obedience from the things he suffered. In this way, God qualified him as a perfect high priest, and he became the source of eternal salvation to all those who obey him."

Jesus was without sin, so what does the Bible mean when it says that he "learned obedience"? John Piper explains:

In all Jesus's suffering, he was being tested. Would he add obedience to obedience until he had grown into the complete, perfect, tested man, that is, the man who had been fully and completely proven and who had responded with perfect obedience, so that he could be described as fully perfected, not meaning that he passed from sinfulness to sinlessness, but that he passed from untested obedience to fully tested obedience.

To walk as sons and daughters of God, we must be willing to partake in the fellowship of His suffering. In 2 Timothy 2:12, apostle Paul explains, "If we suffer, we shall also reign with him. . ." and in Philippians 3:8-11, he makes it personal when he declared: "I want to know Christ and experience the mighty power that raised him from the dead. I want to suffer with him, sharing in his death, so that one way or another I will experience the resurrection from the dead!" Suffering is part of the call to sonship.

Sons and Daughters of God Must Submit to His Discipline: Every father who loves his child, disciplines him. Hebrews 12:5-9 explains: "And have you forgotten the encouraging words God spoke to you as his children? He said, "My child, don't make light of the Lord's discipline, and don't give up when he corrects you. For the Lord disciplines those he loves, and he punishes each one he accepts as his child." As you endure this divine discipline, remember that God is treating you as his own children. Who ever heard of a child who is never disciplined by its father? If God doesn't discipline you as he does all of his children, it means that you are illegitimate and are not really his children at all." Sons and daughters of God humble themselves under the mighty hand of God and submit to His loving discipline.

Proclamation

I am a son/daughter of God. I am an heir of God and a joint heir with Christ. I am led by the Holy Spirit. I am not led by what I see or how I feel. I have faith in God. I believe in my heart and I proclaim with my mouth. Nothing is impossible to me because I believe. I can do all things through Christ. I am self-sufficient, in Chris's sufficiency. I call forth and create my world. I speak life where there is death, order where there is chaos, victory instead of defeat, mercy instead of judgement and love instead of the law. I call forth into my life all the human, material, financial and relational resources that I need to fully accomplish God's plan and purpose for my life. My steps are ordered by the Lord. I am anointed to excel! Amen.

> *Jesus has conquered the devil. Our job it to resist him and shut down his operation in our lives.*

STUDY QUESTIONS

1. The Bible clearly states that God has placed tremendous value in us. In spite of that, so many Christians struggle with fear, self-doubt, and low self-image. Why is that? Do you recognize and own your personal value?

2. What is negative self-talk, and why is it so harmful? Where does it originate? How can we overcome negative self-talk?

3. How can you harness and deploy your creative power to change your life?

4. What is delegated authority? What authority did God delegate to us? How can we exercise it today?

5. Where does the devil get his power? What are his strategies and tricks? How can we stop him? Pool your Bible knowledge and discuss characters in the Bible. How were they tempted by the devil? Did they fail or succeed? What principles helped them to succeed?

6. How can we engage the supernatural realm? Can I contact God using my five senses? Why or why not? What is the importance of speaking in tongues? How can we access all the abundant resources that God has already provided for us in the spirit realm?

7. How can we transition from children into sons? Pool your Bible knowledge as a group and discuss notable Bible characters. Identify instances when they walked as sons and when they acted as children. What was the outcome in each instance?

8. Who are you? Do you know your identity in Christ? Does the devil recognize you as a "son" of God? Why or why not?

SONSHIP PATTERN

Sonship is knowing my position in Christ and walking in it! It means recognizing the nature, attributes, and capabilities of God within you until it moves you to act like God in the earth. When you say "In the name of Jesus," immediately the heavens know what you are saying. You are saying, "I am walking in the pattern. I am a "son" of God, and I come in the rights and authority of sonship."

CHAPTER 4
JESUS, GOD'S SONSHIP PATTERN

Jesus, the Pattern Son

In the olden days, when a person wanted to make a piece of clothing, they bought the pattern. They either did not have stores that sold the clothes already made or where they did, they were expensive. So, there were mail order catalogs that sold the patterns. They would make the outfit and put a photo of the finished product in the catalog, so people can see what the outfit looks like. The point is, if you have the pattern and follow the instructions, you will replicate exactly the style that was advertised. To produce the clothing, people would place the pattern directly on a desired fabric, pin the pattern pieces to the fabric, and then cut around them to produce the style from the fabric, using the pattern as a guide.

Access into the Jesus mold is through identification in Jesus's suffering, death, and resurrection.

God provided a pattern of sonship. Jesus is the pattern. Hebrews 2:10 states:

> God, for whom and through whom everything was made, chose to bring many sons into glory. And it was only right

that he should make Jesus, through His suffering, a perfect leader, fit to bring them into their salvation. So now Jesus and the ones he makes holy have the same Father. That is why Jesus is not ashamed to call them His brothers and sisters.

This scripture outlines God's intent. God wanted to bring many sons into glory, meaning, that He wanted to produce many sons and daughters just like Christ. So, he decided to make a mold, a model or pattern—the sonship mold. His plan was to make Jesus the perfect leader, model, mold, or pattern of a new breed of "sons" who would walk in the glory of God—manifesting all His excellencies, power, authority, and dominion in the earth. Hebrews 2:16 states clearly that this divine plan was not initiated for the benefit of angels, but for us human beings— "the descendants of Abraham." Then God set His plan in motion. First, Jesus had to become flesh and blood, like us. One day God sent the angel Gabriel 'to Nazareth, a village in Galilee, to a young virgin named Mary. She was engaged to be married to a man named Joseph, a descendant of King David (Luke 1:26–27). That began the "sonship pilot," and Jesus launched His rescue mission for humanity that ended on a Roman cross. God's pathway was the cross. Access into the Jesus mold is through identification in Jesus's suffering, death, and resurrection. Once we do that, we are adopted into God's family and become heirs of God and co-heirs with Jesus. We buy into the pattern, and Jesus can legitimately call us His brothers and sisters.

Jesus became the Son of Man to make us "sons" of God!

Paul eloquently describes the exchange transaction that takes place in Galatians 2:20: "I have been crucified with Christ; it is no longer I who live, but Christ lives in me; and the life which I now live in the flesh I live by faith in the Son of God, who loved me and gave Himself for me." We are crucified with Christ, buried with Him by baptism into His death, raised with Him in power, and are now seated with Him in heavenly places, above all principalities and powers.

Jesus Modeled the Sonship Principles

Jesus was the pattern son, and He modeled all the sonship principles. Jesus recognized and owned His personal value. He taught us to call God "Abba." He transitioned us from a relationship to God of master/ servant into a father/son relationship. Jesus knew His source. In John 10:30; He said, I and My Father are one. The Bible is replete with powerful I AM statements that clearly articulated Jesus's conviction as to who He is and what His mission is. He said, "I AM the light of the world" (John 8:12); "I AM the bread of life" (John 6:35); "I AM the way, the truth and the life" (John 14:6), "I AM the door" (John 10:9); "I AM the resurrection and the life" (John 11:25), and more.

Jesus did not look to people for approval. In John 5:41 (NKJV), He said, "I do not receive honor from men." He did not try to convince people of His value or look to them to validate Him. He knew who he was! In John 2:23–25, the Bible states: "Now while he was in Jerusalem at the Passover Festival, many people saw the signs He was performing and believed in His name. But Jesus would not entrust Himself to them, for He knew all people. He did not need any testimony about mankind, for He knew what was in each person." Jesus was free from people! Knowledge of who He was freed Him from human opinions, good or bad, and released Him to be all that God wanted Him to be.

Jesus spoke with authority! He inaugurated His ministry with a bold declaration that left His enemies gasping for breath! Luke 4:18 records the incident:

> When he came to the village of Nazareth, his boyhood home, he went as usual to the synagogue on the Sabbath and stood up to read the Scriptures. The scroll of Isaiah the prophet was handed to him. He unrolled the scroll and found the place where this was written: "The Spirit of the Lord is upon me, for he has anointed me to bring Good News to the poor. He has sent me to proclaim that captives will be released, that the blind will see, that the oppressed will be set free, and that the time of the Lord's favor has come." He rolled up the scroll, handed it back to the attendant, and sat down. All eyes in the synagogue looked at him intently. Then he began to speak to them. "The Scripture you've just heard has been fulfilled this very day!"

He was basically saying, the wait is over; your Messiah is here!

He did not try to fit in. He was not a people pleaser. In John 6:53–67, when many of His disciples deserted His ministry because of His hard teaching, Jesus did not apologize or try to placate them or change His message to accommodate them. On the contrary, He asked the apostles "Are you also going to leave?" one interpretation being, if you too want to leave, here is the door. He knew that He was Jesus, the Son of God, and that was enough! Insightfully, Peter replied "Lord, to whom would we go? You have the words that give eternal life. We believe, and we know you are the Holy One of God."

Jesus modeled the proper exercise of delegated power and authority. He was fully man when He walked on the earth, but He fully manifested as the Son of God and exercised power over all creation. In Matthew 8:26–27, He calmed the sea and walked on water. In John 2:3–17 and Matthew 17 27, He exercised power over nations. He cast out devils, healed the sick and raised the dead. Acts 10:38, summarizes Jesus's exercise of the power delegated to Him by God— "how God anointed Jesus of Nazareth with the Holy Spirit and with power, who went about doing good and healing all who were oppressed by the devil, for God was with Him." Jesus was the Son of man and the Son of God. Son of man because he had a human body, and Son of God because of his source.

In Matthew 8:5–13; we see a vivid illustration of the importance and weight Jesus gave to a proper understanding of delegated authority. The Bible tells of the exchange between Him and a centurion.

> Now when Jesus had entered Capernaum, a centurion came to Him, pleading with Him, saying, "Lord, my servant is lying at home paralyzed, dreadfully tormented." And Jesus said to him, "I will come and heal him." The centurion answered and said, "Lord, I am not worthy that You should come under my roof. But only speak a word, and my servant will be healed. For I also am a man under authority, having soldiers under me. And I say to this *one,* 'Go,' and he goes; and to another, 'Come,' and he comes; and to my servant, 'Do this,' and he does *it."* When Jesus heard *it,* He marveled . . . Then Jesus said to the centurion, "Go your way; and as you have believed, *so* let it be done for you." And his servant was healed that same hour.

The centurion's understanding of authority and delegation impressed Jesus so much that He marveled. It's like He was saying to the centurion "Wow! You get it. I have been trying to teach this to my disciples, and they still don't get it"

Jesus did not empower the devil in His life through His thoughts, words, choices, or relationships. Rather, He overcame him with the Word of God, the sword of the Spirit. Hebrews 4:15 confirms that He faced all of the same testing and temptations we do, yet He did not sin. When the devil tried to steal Jesus's authority by asking Him to bow down and worship him, Jesus rebuked him: "Get out of here, Satan, for the Scriptures say 'you must worship the Lord your God and serve only him'" (Matthew 4:10; NLT). Even in the garden of Gethsemane, when the cross was looming large, the pressure was overwhelming, and the devil was tempting Him to exercise His human will and walk away from the cross, He did not give in, but cried out in anguish "not my will, but yours be done." (Luke 22:42)

Jesus knew that His sonship was his key to the supernatural, so He stayed connected to God the Father at all times. He said in John 10:30, "I and The Father are one." This close knit relationship is evidenced by Jesus's personal commitment to private prayer. The gospel accounts show again and again Jesus going off by Himself to seek God in prayer (Matthew 14:23; Mark 1:35; 6:6; Luke 6:12; 5:16; 9:18; 11:1; John 17). He prayed so much that in Luke 11: 1, His disciples asked Him to teach them how to pray. In John 5:19, when He was being harassed by the Jewish leaders for healing a man on the Sabbath, Jesus said "My Father is always working, and so am I." He continued:

> I tell you the truth, the Son can do nothing by himself. He does only what he sees the Father doing. Whatever the Father does, the Son also does. For the Father loves the Son and shows Him everything he is doing.

Jesus would not settle for less that the Father's will for him. In John 6:14-15, after He fed the five thousand with five loaves and two fish,

He perceived that the crowd wanted to take Him by force to make Him king; so, "He slipped away into the hills by Himself." He would not conform to their expectations. He would not settle for less than God's best.

Jesus was inextricably connected and plugged in to God the Father! He would show Jesus what He wants worked out in the earth, and Jesus would execute it! Instead of starting His own work or "ministry" and asking God to come over and bless His work, Jesus simply found out in prayer what God wanted done in the earth and then joined God where He was already at work. He and God the Father were always on the same page. No wonder He had such a preponderance of supernatural manifestations, miracles, signs, and wonders in His ministry.

> *Jesus simply found out in prayer what God wanted done in the earth and then joined God where He was already at work.*

Jesus did not begin His ministry as a child, either physically or spiritually. The next time we meet Jesus in the scriptures after His birth was when He stayed back in Jerusalem after the Passover celebration (Luke 2:41–52.) He was twelve years old. His parents looked frantically for Him and found Him three days later, sitting in the temple among religious teachers, listening to them, and asking them questions. When His parents chided Him, Jesus's response was, "Didn't you know that I must be in my Father's house?" He spent time learning the Word and growing in the knowledge of God. It is no surprise that we read these words in Luke 2:52: "Jesus grew in wisdom and in stature and in favor with God and all the people." Jesus did not start His ministry as a child, and neither should we. He devoted time to grow and mature as a Son of God. Even His brothers tried, as siblings often do, to goad Him into starting His ministry before He was ready, but Jesus refused.

In John 7:2–9, the Bible states:

> But soon it was time for the Jewish Festival of Shelters, and Jesus's brothers said to him, "Leave here and go to Judea, where your followers can see your miracles! You can't become famous if you hide like this! If you can do such wonderful things, show yourself to the world!" For even his brothers didn't believe in him. Jesus replied, "Now is not the right time for me to go, but you can go anytime. The world can't hate you, but it does hate me because I accuse it of doing evil. You go on. I'm not going to this festival, because my time has not yet come." After saying these things, Jesus remained in Galilee.

Jesus refused to be pressured by people or stampeded by personal pride, wrong motives, or the devil to begin His ministry before He was ready. He waited, trained, learned the Word of God, endured temptation, and learned obedience through suffering. In other words, He went through the process. He grew up! He did not start His ministry until He was ready, and that was not until He was about thirty years old. Think about it! He spent thirty invisible years preparing for a three year ministry. But when it was time, He knew it, hell knew it, and the world knew it too! In Matthew 16:15–16, when He asked His disciples: "Who do you say that I am?" Peter responded without hesitation, "You are the Christ, the Son of the Living God."

In the monotheistic Jewish culture, Peter's declaration was nothing short of shocking! Dan Graves, explains:

> Usually the better we get to know someone, the less perfect we find them. The opposite was true for those who walked with Jesus in the first century. Put yourself in Peter's place. Peter has lived with Jesus for months. He's seen Him tired, hungry, and thirsty; he's seen Him angry; he's heard Him ask questions to gather facts the way any other person does. In other words, Peter has seen Jesus as fully human. In spite of these facts, Peter declares, "You are the Christ the son of the living God."

> "Peter's Jewish contemporaries think of God as high above all highness, pure above all human purity. To be a son of God is to have the character of God. So, for Peter to say this, is to say, "I see in you, Jesus, a moral and spiritual character that puts you on an equal footing with God—a partaker of His nature." (Graves)

Peter was saying—you are walking as a son of God in the earth! Jesus's immediate reaction was to praise Peter: "Blessed are you Simon son of John, for flesh and blood has not revealed this to you but my father who is in heaven" "Peter has recognized a radical truth about Christ's person that millions of Christians have endorsed ever since."

> Soon after Peter's declaration, the Pharisees scheme to have Jesus executed. According to them, Jesus deserves to die because "You being a man make yourself equal to God" John 10:33.

The fact is that the Pharisees discerned the same thing Peter did, but to them it was blasphemy. Jesus's manifestation as a Son of God was inescapable, even to His enemies!

> *Jesus spent thirty invisible years preparing for a three year ministry.*

Jesus: God's Sonship Mold

Jesus is God's sonship mold. Hebrews 1:2–3 states that: Jesus is the firstborn to bring many sons to glory. God wanted to stupefy the world by the simultaneous manifestation of the "sons" of God. Imagine if all the Christians in the world walked in Christ's pattern for just one day—working the works of God, raising the dead, healing the sick, and setting the captives free! The closest example we have of this is in the book of Acts when the apostles were unleashed upon their world after being baptized with the Holy Spirit. In Acts 17:6, they were described by their enemies as the men who have "turned the world upside down."

In a specific instance involving Peter and John, Acts 4:13 reports: "Now when they saw the boldness of Peter and John, and perceived that they were unlearned and ignorant men, they marveled; and they took knowledge of them, that they had been with Jesus." Enough said! That was all the explanation needed. "They had been with Jesus." They are walking in the sonship pattern. What amazed their enemies was that they "were ordinary, ignorant mean." They were not specially gifted, trained, or educated men. In fact, their ordinariness is what confirmed to people that they had been with Jesus.

What this indicates is that everybody qualifies for new covenant sonship. There is no spiritual pedigree or elite qualification. You don't need a college degree or to go to seminary to walk in victory, as a son or daughter of God in the earth. All that is required is obedience and willingness to know God and commit to growth in Christ. In fact, God takes special delight in using the unqualified—men and women who do not meet the standard of human merit or status but who dare to place their faith and trust in Jesus and do what He says.

First Corinthians 1:26–29 is one of my life Bible passages. It states:

> Remember, dear brothers and sisters, that few of you were wise in the world's eyes or powerful or wealthy when God called you. Instead, God chose things the world considers foolish in order to shame those who think they are wise. And He chose things that are powerless to shame those who are powerful. God chose things despised by the world, things counted as nothing at all, and used them to bring to nothing what the world considers important. As a result, no one can ever boast in the presence of God.

> *God takes special delight in using the unqualified—men and women who do not meet the standard of human merit or status.*

Sonship is knowing my position in Christ and walking in it! When you say "In the name of Jesus," immediately the heavens know what you are saying. You are saying, "I am walking in the pattern. I am a "son" of God, and I come in the rights and authority of sonship."

THE PATTERN
"Sons" of God Are Filled with the Holy Spirit

The energy force of the Jesus mold is the Holy Spirit. He is also the seal of our sonship. In Ephesians 1:13-14, the Bible states that "when you believed in Christ, He identified you as His own by giving you the Holy Spirit, whom He promised long ago. The Spirit is God's guarantee that He will give us the inheritance He promised and that He has purchased us to be His own people."

> *The energy force of the Jesus mold is the Holy Spirit.*

We have already studied Romans 8:16–19 that describes how the Holy Spirit indwells us and affirms our adoption into the family of God and our identity as children of God. In Romans 8:11, the Bible states that the same Holy Spirit who raised up Jesus from the dead now dwells in us.

You cannot operate as a "son" of God without the help, tutoring, agency, and partnership of the Holy Spirit. That is why Jesus instructed the apostles to do nothing until they received the Holy Spirit. Wait for Him, Jesus said, because any work done without partnership with the Holy Spirit breaks the sonship mold. It is "strange fire"; fruitless work that will be burned up.

"Sons" of God Have the Image of Christ

The image of a thing is the representation, likeness, or resemblance of that person or thing. Genesis 1:26–27 states that God made us in His image, after His likeness, meaning that we have His nature, attributes, and capabilities. The image of Christ is that He was one with the Father, prayerful, preaching the word and exercising authority, was full of power, lived by faith, embodied righteousness, and always knew and did

> *Sonship means recognizing the nature, attributes, and capabilities of God within me until it moves me to act like God on the earth.*

what the Father did. The image of Christ is sonship. Sonship is knowing your identity in Christ and walking in it! It means recognizing the nature, attributes, and capabilities of God within you until it moves you to act like God in the earth. As a "son" of God, *I am* the spitting image of Christ: I look exactly like Jesus in my spirit. I simply need to believe it and allow what is already in my spirit to manifest through my soul and rule over my body.

"Sons" of God Walk by Faith

Faith is leaning on God with absolute trust and confidence in his power, wisdom and goodness. It is the currency of the kingdom of God, and the legal tender with which to transact in the spirit. "Sons" of God must walk by faith because it is the master key that opens every door in the kingdom. Hebrews 11:1 AMP: states that: "Faith is the assurance, the confirmation and title deed of the things I hope for, being the proof of things that I do not see and the conviction of their reality. Faith perceiving as real fact, what is not revealed to the senses." Faith is critical to walking as a "son" of God in the earth because without faith, it is impossible to please God, because s/he who comes to God must believe that He is and is a rewarder of those who diligently seek Him (Hebrews 11:6).

"Sons" of God Have a Heart of Thanksgiving

Gratitude in the heart, even when there are tears in the eyes, is a mark of mature sons and daughters of God. Trust, peace, contentment and rest grow abundantly in a grateful heart. On the other hand, worry, anxiety, fear and ungodly ambition grow luxuriously in hearts that do not stop, reflect and give thanks. Sons and daughters of God know that even though things may not have turned out as they prayed or expected, they can rest in the knowledge that God is faithful, is at work in their lives, and will make "all things work together for good" (Romans 8:28). An attitude of gratitude elevates their focus, allows them to see the big picture and share the divine perspective. Philippians 4:6-7 (KJV) states: "Be anxious for nothing, but in everything by prayer and supplication, with thanksgiving, let your requests be made known to God, and the peace of God, which surpasses all understanding, will guard your hearts and minds through Christ Jesus." For "sons" of God, gratitude turns what they have into enough.

"Sons" of God Are Not Perfect

Being a "son" of God and walking in the rights and privileges of sonship does not require perfection. But it requires a personal relationship with God and being led by the Holy Spirit (Romans 8:14). Mature sons and daughters of God have victory over the flesh, the devil, the world, and sin; and exercise power over addictions and bad habits. "Sons" of God know their

> *The call to sonship is a call to maturity. It is a call to responsibility, accountability, stewardship, and service.*

Father. That intimate knowledge of the character of God empowers them to do exploits. Daniel 11:32 puts it succinctly. "The people who know their God shall be strong, and do great exploits."

I was talking to a beautiful young woman named Sanae, whose story is in the next chapter. She said to me: "Gloria, I made some wrong choices. I am not perfect." Then she said, "Sons of God are not perfect." She was right. Let's start with the first son of God. The Bible states in Luke 3:38, "Kenan was the son of Enosh, Enosh was the son of Seth, Seth was the son of Adam, Adam was the son of

God." There you have it. Adam, the first man, was the son of God. He was not perfect, and together with his wife, Eve, he chose to transgress the clear command of God and eat the fruit of the tree of knowledge of good and evil, and in so doing plunged mankind into sin. We inherited his sin nature, and none of us was born perfect. Then God sent the last Adam, Jesus, who Himself was also the Son of God. He was the only perfect, sinless person to walk on this planet. The call to sonship is not a call to perfection. Rather, it is a call to maturity. It is a call to responsibility, accountability, stewardship, and service.

Who Are the "Sons" of God?

1. "Sons" of God are men and women who, through understanding of their divine source and nature, release the power and life of God into the world.

2. They are born again Christians who, taking the kingly anointing of authority and the priestly anointing of power, rule and serve in the earth, enforcing the victory of the cross.

3. Being a "son" means recognizing the nature, attributes, and capabilities of God within me, until it moves me to act like God on the earth.

4. The "sons" of God reject sin. They do not condone sin in themselves or others. They have the values, priorities, preferences, and tastes of their Father. They are chips off the old block!

5. "Sons" of God have manifestations. "Sons" of God dominate!

6. "Sons" of God teach principalities and powers the manifold wisdom of God.

7. For "sons" of God, the Bible is the infallible Word of God and the final authority on all questions, issues, and discussions. When life doesn't make sense and they cannot explain their circumstances, "sons" of God cling to the Word of God. They trust the nature and character of God.

"Sons" of God do not use God's resources for personal glory, agenda, or vendetta. "Sons" of God are positive. "Sons" of God build people up and do not tear them down. "Sons" of God treat all people with love and respect because they bear the image of God. "Sons" of God exercise power over addictions and bad habits, and represent the kingdom with excellence, integrity, passion, and dignity. "Sons" of God have victory over the flesh, the devil, the world, and sin.

We Are Sons of God!

Our destiny is sonship. Walk in it, talk like it, and act like it. Choose to walk in the pattern. The rest of this book will present stories of "sons" of God—men and women who walk in the pattern.

Proclamation

I am a son/daughter of God. I am an heir of God and a joint-heir with Christ; therefore, all things are mine! I am an offspring of God and a doer of the word; I am born into greatness. I am a king and priest unto God, and I reign upon the earth. I am anointed to prosper and empowered to succeed. The Lord has given me the power to tread on serpents and scorpions, and over all the power of the enemy: and nothing shall by any means hurt me. I plead the blood of Jesus over my home, children, grandchildren, finances, job, relationships and ministry. I take authority over depression, oppression and bondage. I cancel every plan of the devil to steal, kill and destroy in my life! Amen.

STUDY QUESTIONS

1. Jesus is the pattern son. What is the pattern that He modeled for us? Discuss Bible stories that exemplify Jesus walking as the Son of God.

2. What qualifies you as a son of God? Can everybody qualify for sonship? Discuss Bible examples of God using the most unlikely candidates for an assignment? Name "unqualified" Bible characters whom God used? Discuss present day examples of "unqualified" people that God used.

3. Do I have to be perfect to walk as a son of God in the earth? As a group, discuss the lies and accusations that the devil can use to intimidate us and condemn our walk in the pattern of Christ?

4. Who are the sons of God? Pool your Bible knowledge and discuss men and women who walked as sons of God in the Bible. How well did they fit the profile or characteristics of the sons of God in this chapter?

5. Using dictionaries and reference resources, study the section captioned "Who Are the Sons of God?" Can you identify modern day examples of people who fit the sonship profile?

6. On a scale of 1–10, evaluate yourself on the sonship principles and profile. How do you measure up? Where are your areas of weakness?

7. What are the practical steps you can take to make the sonship profile a reality in your life?

> *God wanted to stupefy the world by the simultaneous manifestation of the "sons" of God.*

MANIFESTATIONS

Here are stories and photos of men and women who applied the principles and walked in the pattern of sonship. The amazing results they experienced is eloquent testimony that the principles and pattern are as effective today as they were when Jesus walked the earth!

CHAPTER 5
MANIFESTATIONS: STORIES AND PHOTOS OF PEOPLE WHO APPLIED THESE PRINCIPLES WITH AMAZING RESULTS

Triumph over Cerebral Palsy
The Story of Matthew Ancona

Matthew is a fun and handsome twenty-one-year-old. Like most young men his age, he likes sports and girls. He loves his family and enjoys spending time with them. Matthew loves to go to the mall. He also loves to travel and go on road trips. He likes to go to the park and to visit with family and friends. He is one of the most delightful people you would ever meet. I don't care how bad you are feeling, running into Matt will make you smile. As soon as he sees you, he breaks out into a glorious smile that says "Great to see you!" And it doesn't matter if he saw you just ten minutes ago; he gets so excited and happy to see you all over again, every time. He makes you feel wanted, loved, and valued! The most wonderful thing about him is that he is an equal opportunity lover! It doesn't matter to him whether you are old or young, tall or short, fat or thin, male or female, Republican or Democrat, evangelical or Pentecostal, black, white, Hispanic, or Asian. He smiles happily at everyone and gives hugs, high fives, and fist bumps freely. Matthew loves unconditionally, freely, and lavishly. He loves like God! He is one of the best ambassadors of God's love you will ever meet. He has expressed abundant laughter, love, and joy since birth. Simply stated, he loves people and he loves the Lord.

Meet Matthew

Matthew's Parents

Wherever you see Matthew, his parents are typically not too far away. His mom, Tracey, usually has a brilliant smile and great attitude, just like Matt. Tracey is an outstanding mom. Always caring and tending to Matt! His dad, Michael, is always there to pick him up and put him in the car or in his wheelchair. I have never seen Matt looking unkempt or untidy. Over the years, I have often thought to myself, "I am sure that caring for Matt is not easy, but Michael and Tracey make it look so easy." They do it in a matter-of-fact sort of way, smiling and chatting casually. Their attitude says "Matthew is a gift, not a burden." What impressed me most is that Matt is up and about. He goes to school, he goes to Sunday school, he goes to the mall, and he goes on road trips. He travels wherever he pleases. He is a normal kid, except that he is in a wheelchair. I thought to myself,

"He has great parents; they are proud of their boy, and he knows it, too." Matt is popular. Often, he is surrounded by a crowd of fans; smiling widely, he shakes hands, gives out hugs, high fives, and fist bumps as he makes his way through the crowd. You would think he was a politician running for Congress, except that for Matt, every interaction is pure and genuine, and he is not looking for a vote or anything in return. You can't help but smile as you watch Matthew being Matthew.

Matthew sailing with his dad and playing on the swing with his mom

Matthew's parents are Michael and Tracey Ancona. They met in Virginia in their twenties. Michael was in the Navy and was stationed in Norfolk, Virginia. Both he and Tracey were committed Christians. He attended First Assembly of God Church while Tracey went to Rock Church. They met at church youth programs, dated for three months, and were engaged for a year. They obeyed God and patiently waited on his direction regarding their wedding. God honored their obedience and provided miraculously for large portions of their wedding. They have been married for twenty seven years. Today, they are dedicated Christians who have a passionate commitment to serving the Lord. They are committed in their local church and serve in various ministries.

I admire the Ancona family. Over the years, I have thought to myself, "This is an amazing family. I wonder what happened." If you are like me, you may have asked the same question. Well, I reached out to Tracey and Michael, and they told me their story. It is a story of great faith under fire; the unquestionable supremacy and immutability of the Word of God; the unmitigated power of fervent, faith-filled prayer; and God's miraculous, grace-filled answer. It is a story that will cause your faith to rise and stand straight up! This is their story:

The Ancona Family

Matthew's Birth

When Tracey got pregnant with Matthew, she and Michael knew from early on that the pregnancy might be difficult. She had a childhood kidney issue that was a concern of the doctors who worried whether her kidneys would be able to handle the extra strain of a growing child in her womb. As the pregnancy progressed, her body was retaining a great deal of fluid. On September 24, 1997, at 28.5 weeks of gestation, Tracey went to her doctor's office for a routine prenatal visit. The doctor took one look at her and immediately transferred her into the hospital. She was in the late stages of preeclampsia, and little Matthew was dying inside her. Preeclampsia is a dangerous condition that can occur during pregnancy. It is marked by high blood pressure in women who haven't had high blood pressure previously. It also leads to a high level of protein in the urine and swelling in the feet, legs, and hands.

Tracey called her husband at work and told him the devastating news. Michael left work immediately, stopped by their house to change clothes, and headed to the hospital. Before he left the house, he called his friend Tommy from work. Cell phones were not as common as they are today, and Michael did not have a cell phone. He really only had time for one phone call and that call had to count. There were a lot people Michael could have called, but he chose to call Tommy because he knew that Tommy was a strong, covenant-minded believer. They had spent much time together working shift work and had had lots of conversations. Michael knew he could trust Tommy to stand with him in faith and prayer. For this crisis, he needed the kind of man who would not waver at the promises of God. Tommy was that guy! So, Michael told Tommy what was going on and left for the hospital.

Michael describes his trip to the hospital "The ride to the hospital was agonizing. It was like the devil was in the passenger seat, screaming at me the whole way. "I'll kill your whole family today!" All I could do in response was to praise God and pray in the spirit. Walking into the hospital room and seeing Tracey lying in that bed brought me to the breaking point. I collapsed in her arms, and we both started sobbing uncontrollably. This was the low point, the point where the valley seemed to be the deepest."

> *Access into the Jesus mold is through identification in Jesus's suffering, death, and resurrection.*

Soon after Michael's arrival, the doctor came in to explain what was happening and the immediate next steps. He told Michael that "Tracey's body is rejecting the baby. Her kidneys can no longer handle the extra burden of the pregnancy. Matthew has to be born as soon as possible." In situations like this, the doctors try to improve the baby's chances of survival by giving their lungs a steroid shot, which they did for Matthew. Preferably, they would like to wait for twenty four hours after the steroid shot before delivery, but in this case, there was no time for that. Tracey was wheeled into the operating room right away for an emergency C-section to deliver Matthew. Michael was in the operating room with her. He describes what happened: "I can still see the moment Matthew was pulled out of Tracey's womb. He was purplish and almost had a look of bewilderment. They put him in a small transport gurney and took him to another room. They escorted me in there, and when I entered, I witnessed them giving him CPR. I wasn't allowed to stay, but they did give me enough time to say a few words to him. So, I said 'Hey, Buddy! This is Dad. I see you decided to show up a little early. Listen, Daddy needs to take care of a few things . . . so I'm going to leave you here with these folks; but don't worry because I'll be back." With that, I was escorted out of the room.'"

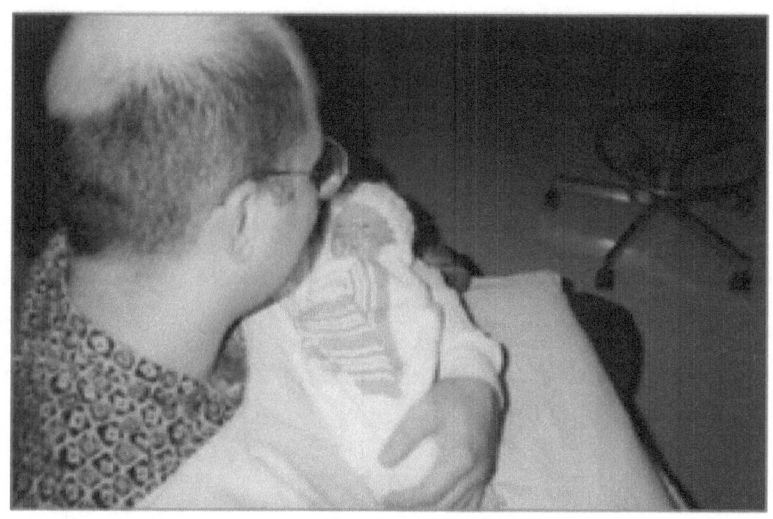

Baby Matthew held by his dad.

Spiritual Warfare

Soon, Tracey's family began to arrive and the call went out to prayer warriors to start praying. The hospital had a chapel, which Michael figured was as good a place as any to wage spiritual warfare for his family. After praying in the chapel for a little while, the surgeons summoned Michael for a status update. The prognosis was as follows: "Matthew had no chance of survival, and Tracey had a very high probability that she would not survive, either." Things did not look good. While waiting for Tracey to be transferred from the post-operation area to a room, Michael went back to the chapel to pray. Michael describes his state of mind: "When things like this happen, how and what you pray about become very important. When your family's life is hanging in the balance, you need to be sure of what the will of the Lord is before you even start to pray. Prayers like, 'Please heal Matthew' or 'Please heal Tracy' are a waste of time.

> *When your family's life is hanging in the balance, you need to be sure of what the will of the Lord is before you even start to pray.*

You need to know what the Word of God says and declare it boldly. God had already provided a covenant of healing through the stripes of Jesus, and it was time to enforce that covenant. My time spent in the chapel consisted of either praying in the spirit, praising God, or declaring His Word. I was joined off and on by family and friends, and we were all praying with the same mind."

Later that evening, Tracey was moved to a room. She was unconscious, with tubes draining fluid from her body. She had to lose thirty pounds of fluid! She was alive, but the doctors warned Michael that she might very well die during the night. With Matthew in the neo-natal intensive care unit (NICU), Michael decided to focus on his wife for the rest of the night. They had a book called *Healing Promises*, published by Kenneth Copeland ministries. It is a collection of all the Bible verses on healing. They also had a CD of healing praise music. With these two instruments of spiritual warfare, Michael settled in for the night in Tracey's room. He spent the whole night reading the healing verses out loud while the CD was playing. Michael explains: "I'm not sure how many times I got through the entire book, but my guess is that it was at least three times. Morning came and miraculously, both Tracey and Matthew had survived the night. I went home to get a few hours of sleep and returned as soon as I could. By the time I got back to the hospital, Tracey's prognosis had improved dramatically. The current outlook was that she would recover. Matthew, however, was a different story. He was not doing well at all. Many of his organs were not working. He was on a ventilator. The doctors told me I could go back to the NICU to see him, so I did. I took one look at him and realized I had made a mistake in coming back to the NICU. He didn't look real. When I saw him the day before, he had just been born. One day later, he was unrecognizable. I told myself that I was not going to come back to the NICU again until his situation was resolved. I knew that it was not going to drag on for a long time. He was either going to live or die within the next forty eight to seventy two hours.

> *I will walk with the Lord in the land of the living.*

Because of this, I knew that seeing him in that state with my physical eyes was not going to inspire faith, but doubt. I left the NICU and went back to the chapel to resume from where I had left off."

God Speaks

Once again, the chapel was the "war room." By this time, reinforcements had arrived. Tracey's dad had driven up from Georgia and joined Michael in the chapel. They continued to praise God for His faithfulness to His Word. Michael had his Bible and was reading the Psalms. As he read Psalm 116, verse 9 jumped out at him. It said, "I will walk with the Lord in the land of the living." That verse hit Michael with a jolt. He explains: "I knew the Lord was speaking to me. He was saying that this was Matthew's verse, and that I could take this as His promise that he was going to live. At that moment, I knew he was going to make it. Now, there was no physical evidence that anything had improved. In fact, you could even say he was getting worse. But I knew right then and there, that this was going to end with him living. The attitude in the chapel changed, and we collectively began to declare that scripture. We shared it with those outside the chapel who were also praying.

Soon, people all over were declaring Psalm 116:9 over Matthew. As Friday became Saturday, our confidence grew. The doctors held a completely different view of Matthew. They were adamant that Matthew had little to no chance of survival. He had too much going against him. His kidneys were not functioning, so he couldn't process any fluid. This limited their ability to give him the medicine he needed. They were doing the best they could, but they were running out of time. The only problem with their point of view is that Matthew refused to die. I felt bad for the doctors because they were bound to what they were seeing in the physical sense. They didn't have the luxury of knowing what we knew—that God had promised that Matthew would live."

Michael spent Saturday alternating between praying in the chapel and visiting Tracey. That evening, he and the other family members and friends went out to dinner. The mood was joyful. A few days before, almost everybody was crying and sad over what was happening. Very few people were really committed to believing God's word. But as time went on, more and more people were coming on board the "believing" train. Every minute that Matthew lived was a confirmation that the devil was losing ground.

Enforcing the Word

Michael went home Saturday night confident, joyful, and in full anticipation that God was true to His promise. He returned on Sunday morning and went straight to Tracey's room. By this time, she was in full recovery mode. She was awake and coherent. She was having breakfast when the doctors came in with some more bad news about Matthew. They said, "Matthew's kidneys are just not working. We can't give him enough medicine because his body can't process it. He will not survive beyond this morning." They were defeated and at the end of their rope. They brought with them some papers for Michael and Tracey to sign. They said "Please sign these documents. This will give us permission to keep his heart pumping after he dies, so that we can have enough time to bring you two down to the NICU to say goodbye to him while he is still technically alive.'"

Michael describes what happened next: "I looked at the doctor with the love of the Lord and gave him my response: 'Doctor, we appreciate all the work you are doing for Matthew; we really do. I'm not a non-intelligent man. I realize that this situation looks pretty dire, especially to you. All your training and all your expertise is telling you Matthew is a lost cause. You are doing all you know to do, and it's not working. But if you will allow me, I am going to tell you a story about something I know. In the twenty seventh chapter of the book of Acts, the Bible tells the story of how the apostle Paul was put on a ship and set sail for Rome. While on that trip, they encountered a terrible storm. The storm raged for days. During that time, the sailors did everything their training taught them to do when a ship was in a storm. They girded the hull with cables, they threw the cargo overboard, and discarded much of the ship's equipment. Eventually, the crew lost all hope that they would be saved.

At that time, Paul made this statement in verses 21 through 25:

> 'Men, you should have listened to me and not have sailed from Crete and incurred this disaster and loss. And now I urge you to take [f]heart, for there will be no loss of life among you, but only of the ship. For there stood by me this night an angel of the God to whom I belong and whom I serve, saying, 'Do not be afraid, Paul; you must be brought

before Caesar; and indeed, God has granted you all those who sail with you.' Therefore, take heart, men, for I believe God that it will be just as it was told me.'"

Michael continued "Doctor, just like the men in this story, you have done all you know to do and it's not working. You have lost all hope that Matthew will live. But I will say to you what Paul said to the sailors on that ship: Be of good cheer because I believe God. Matthew is going to live because God told me he would. I know it doesn't look like that to you. You don't understand why I would say this, and I don't expect you to. Just know that while you are at the end of your rope, God is just getting started. So please, go back to the NICU and keep doing what you're doing. We will not be signing anything because Matthew is not going to die." With that, the doctors left us alone and went back to the NICU."

Breakthrough!

The rest of that Sunday came and went with not much change. Matthew still had not improved; however, more importantly, he still had not died. Michael decided to go back to the house for some rest, so he kissed Tracey goodbye and went back home. He was home for a while when the phone rang. It was Maureen, one of their closest friends. She called from the hospital to tell him that Matthew had finally peed. During this ordeal, two of Matthew's grandmothers came over to pray for him during their lunch hour. Joyce, one of his grandmothers, was praying over him, when she noticed the cotton turn yellow. Contrary to the expectation of the doctors, Matt's kidneys have kicked in and are functioning! Tears of joy rolled down Michael's face. He knew they had won; God had won! This is the triumph of faith. They had stood on the Word of God in faith and had overcome death.

> *They had stood on the Word of God and had overcome death.*

From that moment on, Matthew began to improve. The doctors warned that he was still not out of the woods yet. His kidney function needed to improve and increase. Michael asked the doctors how much pee is needed to certify that his kidneys were okay. First, they said 7 cc (a little less than one-half ounce) and then 21 cc and on and on until they stopped counting. Whatever pee amount they wanted, God supplied it! Finally, they came to agree with God's prognosis that Matthew shall live and not die. He still faced a multitude of challenges, but from that day forward, he made slow

Matthew with grandmas Joyce and Sandra

but steady progress. He was born on September 24, weighing 1 pound, 9 ounces. He left the hospital on December 15 weighing 3 pounds 15 ounces. He was on oxygen when he left. He had rickets and a hernia that would eventually require surgery to correct.

Matthew Is a Winner!

Matthew is a fighter! He fought to stay alive in the womb, he fought to stay alive when the doctors gave up on him, and he fought to stay alive when all the odds were against him. And he won! He is still fighting today, fighting to overcome the damage inflicted by his violent entry into this world. He has cerebral palsy and cannot walk. He is limited in many of the things that most people take for granted. But Matthew is alive and has been for twenty one years now. He is a trophy of God's amazing grace and power, an eloquent testimony to what happens when people trust God and believe His Word.

Matthew

Michael sums it up: "Not long after we brought Matthew home from the hospital, a good friend of mine and I were talking about that first weekend. We were discussing how Matthew managed to survive despite all of the impossible odds he faced. One of the things my friend called to mind was that during that time, during those critical first seventy two hours when nothing seemed to be going right, we never made provision for failure. We would not and did not entertain thoughts of "What if God doesn't come through?" We stood on His Word, without wavering. It was all we had, so it was all we did. Having done all to stand, we stood there; expecting God's word to be true, and it was. Today, twenty one years later, Matthew is still walking with the Lord in the land of the living!

Key Scripture God Used to Strengthen the Ancona Family

Psalm 116:9: "I will walk with the Lord in the land of the living."

Sonship Principles

Matthew's story models the following sonship principles:

1. Jesus gave every believer the power to transact kingdom business in His name and as His representative. The name of Jesus is His signet ring! It entitles us to everything that Jesus has and is. When we use the name of Jesus, we are Christ's representative, presenting *all* that Jesus is! Nothing in heaven, on the earth, beneath the earth, in this world, or the world to come can stop or stand against the mighty name of Jesus!

2. God has placed tremendous value in us, all of us— He calls us sons and daughters! We are the children of God. We are heirs of God and joint heirs with Christ. We have the DNA of God. We are partakers of his divine nature. We are of inestimable value. The value of a thing is measured by how much people are willing to pay for it. Jesus gave His life for us, and that defines our value as sons of God.

3. Owning my personal value allows me to be authentic. God wants me to be authentic. He made me an original. I must be comfortable in my own skin. I am an uncommon package, with my issues, challenges, personality, quirks, skin color, ethnicity, and so forth. I was uniquely put together by God and assigned a unique identifier— my fingerprint. Nothing about me is an accident. Authenticity is God's permission to be what he designed me to be.

4. "Death and life are in the power of the tongue." When we speak death or say unbiblical things, we employ the devil. When we speak forth life and the Word of God, we employ angels. Psalm 103:20–21 tells us that when we give voice to the Word of God, angels perk up their ears. It is their calling card. Once the Word of God is spoken, the angels hasten to execute the spoken word.

> *They never made provision for failure.*

5. In order to take control over my life, I must begin to speak like I created the earth. I am not going to tolerate debt, sickness, and so on in my life. I am going to change things with the words of my mouth, like God did in creation. When we speak and continue to speak the Word of God, we will shut the door in the face of the devil and transform everything around us to conform to the spoken word.

6. Simply stated, the Word of God coming out of my mouth in faith is the most potent weapon known to man. What this means is that every word I speak is on assignment. Once I believe the Word in my heart and launch it forth via the spoken word, it will not return empty; it will achieve its creative purpose and assignment. It is unstoppable!

7. Sons and daughters of God refuse to settle for a life that is beneath their inheritance, no matter, how long and tedious the struggle. This principle is based on the premise that you cannot change what you tolerate. It is a principle that does require strong personal discipline and a great view of God. "Sons" of God believe that God is who He says that He is, and that He would do exactly what He says that He would do. So, they don't negotiate, compromise or settle with the

devil, their flesh, or their circumstances. They stand resolute on the word of God, even if they stand alone. They refuse to make room for, cohabit with or accommodate sickness, sin, failure, bondage, poverty and anything else that is beneath who they are in Christ.

8. You and I have a choice in every situation we face, to act as a son or as a child. Sonship takes faith and requires obedience to the Holy Spirit. A good indicator of whether or not you are a son is in your mind—how you think and what voice you follow. If you are ruled by your emotions, you are a child. If you cater to your flesh, you are a child. If you are led by your five senses, you are a child. If you know what is right to do but choose to act based on how you feel, you are a child.

9. For sons and daughters of God, the Bible is the infallible Word of God and the final authority on all questions, issues, and discussions When life doesn't make sense and they cannot explain their circumstances, "sons" of God cling to the Word of God. They trust the nature and character of God.

> *For sons of God, the Bible is the infallible Word of God and the final authority on all questions, issues, and discussions.*

The story of Matthew teaches us that our God never makes mistakes, and He is faithful to His Word. Matthew is a true gift to the world! Unfortunately, we live in a society where some people think that kids like Matt should not have the right to life in the womb or anywhere else. Well, Matt shatters that lie and puts them all to shame! The Ancona family challenges you and me to be winners. They are saying to us: you can win regardless of the hand that you've been dealt. They inspire me to engage life with love, joy, and a thankful heart, regardless of what life throws at me! They teach us that whatever you are going through today, you can choose to trust God regardless of your circumstances. The promises of God are sure, and we cannot allow our circumstances to redefine the Word of God. Our circumstances may come and go, but the Word of God is the eternal truth period—Amen.

> *Sons of God refuse to settle for less than their inheritance, no matter how long and tedious the struggle.*

Miracle Deliverance and Healing
The Story of Sanae Ahumada
and Linda Udischas

She is a beautiful and vivacious young woman in the prime of her life. It is the week before Christmas. She had just finished her first semester of college with excellent grades and decided to go on a road trip with friends to celebrate. That was when tragedy struck! Her name is Sanae Ahumada, and this is her story!

Sanae lived with her mom, stepdad, and brother in Newark, Delaware. On December 20, 2012, she was involved in a ghastly head-on collision with a tractor-trailer in Atlanta, Georgia. That day forever changed her life. But in a miraculous display of God's amazing grace and power, what should have been a fatal tragedy turned into endless miracles of divine deliverance and healing.

Prologue

The story begins in August 2012, four months before the accident. Sanae was driving her dream car, a new silver Nissan Altima. As she was leaving an event late one evening with a friend, they heard bottles breaking behind them. Sanae was startled and thought that someone may be throwing bottles at her car or that a fight may have broken out in the parking lot, she turned her head to look. Unfortunately, she failed to apply the brakes. Even though she was going only about seven miles per hour, the right front tire of her beloved car rolled over a six inch curb in the parking lot. The air bags were deployed, and the engine immediately stalled. Several days later, the insurance company informed her that the engine, transmission, and radiator twisted when she ran over the curb, and her car was completely totaled. Sanae was devastated! And she was angry with God. How

> *She did not return from that trip until a month later, and she returned a changed woman!*

could He allow this to happen? She felt abandoned and alone.

Where was God when she needed Him? Well, when it came time to look for a new car, Sanae decided to look for something bigger, more truck-like, so that if she ever ran over another curb, the car would not be destroyed, like her Altima. So, she purchased a Ford Escape. This singular act turned out to be a significant contributor to her survival, four months later.

Road Trip

Fast forward to December; Sanae was back from college on Christmas break. She was driving her new Ford Escape and decided to take a road trip to Atlanta, Georgia. Her plan was to leave early on Sunday morning, December 16, and return on Friday, December 21, in time for Christmas. Well, her plans were overtaken by events tragically out of her control. She did not return from that trip until a month later, and she returned a changed woman!

When she told her mom, Linda, that she was planning to drive to Atlanta, Linda immediately opposed the idea for several reasons: it was too far, it was a week before Christmas, and it was winter. But Sanae was twenty two years old and was determined to make the trip. Since Linda couldn't stop her, she insisted that Sanae not drive alone or with only her female friend. If she wanted to go on the trip, she had to find a male friend that her mom trusted to drive with her. It didn't take Sanae long to find a male friend whose sister lives in

Atlanta and who was willing to ride along and visit his family. He joined Sanae and her female friend on the road trip.

On Sunday morning, Sanae and her friends left for Atlanta. They arrived safely, late on Sunday night. On Monday and Tuesday, they went sight-seeing and had a lot of fun. On Wednesday, the nineteenth, Sanae called her mom to tell her about her day. She mentioned that she was going out with her friends one last time that evening. Linda told her that it was a good idea not to go out on Thursday evening so she could get a good night's sleep before the drive home on Friday. She told Sanae to be safe, smart, and have a good time.

The Accident

Sanae describes that fateful day: "I was having a great time in Atlanta. The day before the accident, my friends and I visited the Atlanta Aquarium and did the usual tourist activities. It would be our last night to go out and have a little fun before hitting the road for the long drive back to Delaware. I was hesitant to go out on Wednesday night because I was tired from the busy day, but my friends urged me to have one last night out. We had a great time! The last thing I remember was leaving the club and walking to my car. It was very cold and windy. I woke up two weeks later in the surgical intensive care unit at Atlanta's Grady Hospital."

Back in Delaware, December 19 was a normal day for the Udischas family. After a full day, Linda went to bed at about 10 p.m. At about 2:45 am Thursday, December 20, Linda woke up abruptly from sleep. She sensed that there is a critical need to pray and she asked the Lord who she was to pray for. He told her to pray for Sanae. She didn't think anything of it because she always prays for her children. So, without any hesitation or anxiety, she began to pray for her daughter. She prayed that no weapon formed against her shall prosper, that God would send angels to encamp around her, that the blood of Jesus would cover her and protect her, that no evil would befall her, and no disaster would come near her. As Linda prayed, she began to fall back to sleep, but she was jolted wide awake. She felt as if someone shook her and told her to continue to pray for Sanae. So, she prayed for several more minutes before falling back to sleep.

Sanae's Car after the accident

A Mother's Nightmare

When she woke up on Thursday morning, Linda remembered praying for Sanae in the wee hours of the morning, but she didn't think anything of it. December 20 was a normal morning, and things were going pretty well until 8:15 a.m. when Linda received a text message from Sanae's phone. The text message read, "Linda, please call me. Please." She stared at the message and thought, "This is not Sanae. My daughter does not call me Linda, and she

> *She was jolted awake. She felt as if someone shook her and told her to continue to pray for Sanae.*

doesn't beg me to call her." She had a sinking feeling. Her throat dropped to the pit of her stomach, and her heart began to pound. She called Sanae's phone, and a young woman answered. It was the sister of the young man who rode to Atlanta with Sanae. She told Linda that Sanae was in a horrible accident with a tractor-trailer, was currently in surgery, and that Linda needed to get to Grady Hospital in Atlanta as soon as possible. Linda was beside herself! All she could say was, "No, no, no, no . . ." over and over. Jamesia, the young woman, begged her to stop screaming; she gave Linda the name of the nearest airport, the name and phone number of the hospital, and Sanae's emergency code name. Linda immediately called the hospital, and they told her the same thing, that Sanae was still in surgery and that she needed to make arrangements to get to Atlanta as soon as possible. Linda immediately called her husband, Rick, to tell him the horrible news. She asked him to come home right away and take her to the airport. Rick worked five minutes from home, so she had enough time to throw a few things into a duffle bag and wake up their son, Aaron. She calmly told him that his sister was in an auto accident and she had to go to Atlanta.

As soon as Rick came home, Linda jumped into the car, and they headed for the airport. As they were driving to the Philadelphia airport, Linda began to call people to pray for Sanae. She called their church, friends, and family. At this point, Rick reminded her that she needed to call the airlines and book a flight. She called American Airlines and was told that no seat was available that day.

She proceeded to call United Airways and Southwest Airlines, with the same result. No seat was available on any plane to Atlanta. This was the Thursday before Christmas, and the entire weekend flight schedule was fully booked by holiday travelers. Then she called Delta Airlines. The agent told her that there is one flight out of Philadelphia Airport to Atlanta that day at 2:15 p.m., and there are only two seats left. Linda hesitated! She didn't want to wait until the afternoon. She thought "I need to get to Atlanta as soon as possible. I need to be on a plane now, and 2:15 p.m. is too late" The Delta sales agent cut through her fog. She told Linda in a clear, crisp, urgent, and firm tone that if she didn't book a seat at that moment, she would not be leaving Philadelphia that day. Linda booked the flight. It was 9 a.m., and the flight would not leave until five hours later. Rick and Linda turned around to go back home and wait. Linda felt defeated. She felt as if she was letting her daughter down, that when Sanae needed her the most, she could not be there for her. She felt so helpless and wept bitterly! Through her tears, she began to thank God for giving her such a beautiful daughter for twenty two years. And she gave Sanae back to Him.

Shortly after arriving home, she received a phone call from Grady Hospital. It was Dr. Nicholas, the emergency room trauma surgeon. He explained that his team was finishing up with Sanae's surgery and that she would soon be in recovery. He then went on to tell Linda about Sanae's injuries. First, he told her that Sanae's intestines had ruptured in the accident, and they had removed half of her large intestine and part of her small intestine. Linda thought, "Okay, she may need a colostomy bag. We can live with that." Next, Dr. Nicholas explained that she has a fracture to her C2. The C2 vertebra, also known as the axis, is the second uppermost vertebra in the spine and supports the head. Linda thought, "Okay, fractures heal. We can live with that." She didn't know at that time that a fracture of the C1 or C2 vertebrae were usually fatal or could paralyze the individual. Finally, Dr. Nicholas informed Linda that Sanae had a subarachnoid hematoma, or brain bleed. That's when Linda lost it! She knew how terribly serious a brain injury could be. She fell to a crumpled heap on the floor and wept desperately with deep, heaving sobs.

It was now about 10:30 a.m. Linda was anxious to get to the airport. She couldn't afford to miss her flight. She asked Rick to take her back to the airport to wait for the flight. While Rick was driving back to the Philadelphia airport, Linda began to make more phone calls to gather as many prayer warriors as possible. When they arrived at the airport, Rick and Linda said their goodbyes with

> *She realized that she had stepped into the realm of the supernatural.*

big hugs and tears. As Linda walked into the airport, it seemed as if everything and everyone around her froze and was in slow motion. It was the strangest feeling she had ever had, like something out of a movie. She realized later that she had stepped into the realm of the supernatural.

Linda's Vision

She was three hours early for her flight. As she approached her departure gate, she immediately began to look for an outlet to charge her phone. She couldn't allow her phone to die; it was her lifeline to the hospital. The airport was packed with holiday travelers, and every outlet was taken. Just then she spotted one across the room and dashed toward it. She plugged her phone into the outlet and sat down with a sigh of relief. Then she looked up and noticed a woman sitting a few rows away from her. She slowly recognized her as a woman named Cheryl from church. Cheryl recognized her as well and came over. She sat next to Linda and said, "Linda, are you alright? You don't look so well." Linda told her about Sanae and that she was on her way to Grady Hospital in Atlanta. Cheryl was also going to Atlanta to visit her parents for Christmas. She asked Linda how she planned to get to the hospital from the airport. "By taxi," Linda replied. Cheryl, then called her father and asked if he would be able to drive Linda to the hospital, and he agreed. Cheryl prayed with Linda. Then she sat and waited with her until boarding time. She assured Linda that she would be waiting for her when she got off the plane in Atlanta.

Linda boarded, found her row, squeezed into her middle seat and got ready for takeoff. She put her ear buds in, turned on worship music, and closed her eyes. She needed to focus on Jesus. She needed to worship Him. As she was silently worshiping and praying for Sanae, she heard the Holy Spirit say, "Lift your hands and worship Me." She thought, "No, I can't do that. The people next to me will think I'm crazy!" She opened her eyes and took a peek at her seat mates. She closed her eyes again and continued to worship. Again, came the voice; "Lift your hands and worship Me." So, Linda lifted her hands halfway, pretending as if she was yawning and quickly lowered them back on her lap. There, she did it! She had lifted her hands in worship. But the voice of the Lord came again to her; "No. Lift your hands and worship Me." Linda knew she had to obey. She thought to herself, "Who cares; I don't know these people anyway!" So, she lifted her hands as far as she could and began to worship God. All of a sudden, she had a vision! She saw Sanae lying in a dark room. She looked so beautiful and peaceful. Then Jesus walked into this pitch-black room. He turned to look at Linda and gave her a look that said, "Watch this!" He then went and stood beside Sanae and began to lay His hands on her, and everywhere He rested His nail-pierced hands, He left His blood. He started at her head, then her neck, her shoulders, her belly, her legs, and finally her feet. She was literally covered with His bloody handprints. At that moment, Linda knew that her daughter would be okay.

As the plane approached Atlanta, Linda began to panic about getting to the hospital. She knew Cheryl had checked bags and would need to go to baggage claim. She only had a carry-on bag and had planned on running straight for a taxi to go to the hospital. She knew Cheryl meant well and wanted to help, but she didn't have time to wait at baggage claim. So, she decided that she would thank Cheryl and tell her that she would prefer to catch a cab and head straight for the hospital. However, the Lord told her to take the ride from Cheryl's father. When the plane landed in Atlanta, Cheryl was waiting for Linda at the gate. As they headed for baggage claim. Linda kept thinking to herself, "I don't have time for this, Lord!" Cheryl's father met them on their way to baggage claim and when they go there, her bags were already on the carousel. Linda was relieved. They headed to the parking garage. Again, Linda was thinking "I don't have time for this, Lord. I need to be heading to the airport!" Before she could finish her thought, Cheryl's dad popped open the trunk of a beautiful new Bentley! Linda was so humbled and blessed to think that the Lord not only arranged a friend for her at the airport, but also arranged for her to be driven to the hospital in style! Our God is an amazing, wonderful, good, good Father!

Grady Hospital

As Linda entered the seventh floor surgical intensive care unit at Grady Hospital, she was met by Jamesia, the young lady who had texted her at 8:15 in the morning. Jamesia led her to Sanae's room. As the large double doors opened and they stepped through, Linda looked to her right and saw Sanae. Her beautiful daughter was bruised, cut, beaten, and hooked up to a multitude of machines. Linda froze! She couldn't move. She stood and stared at her daughter in horrified disbelief. Jamesia gently pulled her into the room. She wrapped her hand around Sanae's hand and told her, "Mommy's here. Mommy's here." As Linda sat next to her daughter, taking in the enormity of the situation, the condition of Sanae's body from head to toe, and all the machines, wires, and tubes coming in and out of her limp body, she heard the Holy Spirit tell her to take a picture of Sanae. Once again, Linda politely argued with the Lord. She said, "Lord, no! I don't want this to be my last memory of her!" He responded, "It is not so you can remember her like this, it is so she can see where I have taken her from." Once again Linda was reassured, and she took the picture.

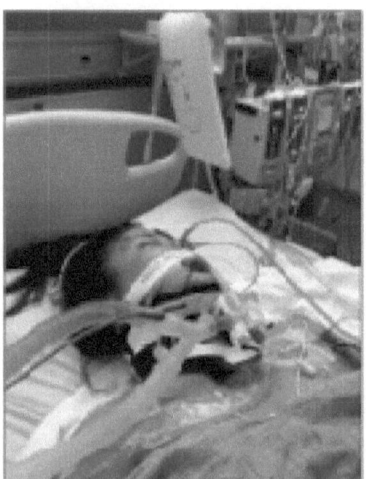

Linda's first photo of Sanae at Grady hospital

Jamesia told Linda about the events of the evening as she knew them. Sanae was not drunk, but she was tired as she drove her friend Ashlee and Jamesia's brother, Bryant, to a local convenience store after leaving the club. That was when she had the head-on collision with the tractor-trailer. Ashlee and Bryant were both miraculously delivered. They were treated and released that evening.

Shortly after her arrival at Grady Hospital, Dr. Nicholas came to Sanae's room to speak to Linda. Here's Linda's recollection of that discussion: After going over her injuries and the surgical procedures, he said that if she survives, she may have permanent brain damage or be paralyzed from the neck down. The next twenty four to forty eight hours were the most critical. They would take her back down in twenty four hours for a CT scan of her brain to check on the bleeding. If she was still bleeding, they would have to operate to release the pressure on her brain. He told Linda that they had done all they could possibly do, and now they just had to wait. Linda thanked Dr. Nicholas for all he and his team had done and told him that her God will now take over! She immediately texted the update to her husband and the prayer warriors and asked them to pray specifically for the brain bleeding to cease.

God's Miracles

The next morning, they performed the CT scan of Sanae's brain. Several hours later, Dr. Nicholas gave Linda the good news. The bleeding had stopped, and surgery was no longer necessary! This was *Miracle No. 1!*

Next, they needed to determine the extent of injury to her C2. For that, she needed to be off the ventilator, so they could do an MRI of

> "It is not so you can remember her like this, it is so she can see where I have taken her from."

her neck. They reduced the dosage of her coma-inducing medicines to wake her up, so they can assess her limbs. She woke up in a panic. The nurse quieted her down and calmly told her that she was in the hospital. The doctor then asked her if she could do a thumbs up. She did two thumbs up! Next, they asked if she could wiggle her toes. She moved both her feet! The room broke into joyful applause! Sanae was not paralyzed! She understood and followed commands! This was *Miracle number 2!*

It was day eight, and Sanae was still not able to breathe on her own. She was still in a medically induced coma, and then she developed pneumonia. Linda immediately began calling for prayer. She went into the family lounge to make some calls while her friend Debbie Sullivan stayed with Sanae. After the phone calls, Linda turned on worship music and began to worship. God's presence became so manifest in the room that Linda called Debbie to come to the lounge right away to worship with her. It was beautiful! As they worshiped, a gentleman entered the lounge, and Linda asked him politely to be quiet. She closed her eyes for a few minutes and when she opened them, she saw Debbie lying prostrate on the floor in worship, and the gentlemen who had just entered was on his knees, arms raised to heaven, with tears streaming down his face. It was a gloriously beautiful moment in the presence of Almighty God.

The next day, Sanae was successfully removed from the ventilator, and she began to breathe on her own! On day ten, she was sitting up in a chair and eating ice chips. It was a great time of rejoicing! It was also time to take Sanae for an MRI of her neck to see the extent of the fracture to her C2. The results came back positive.

Only the odontoid process, or tip of her C2 vertebrae, had fractured and chipped off. No surgery would be required! She would only have to wear a neck brace for six weeks. This was *Miracle No 3!*

On day eleven, Sanae took a turn for the worse. Linda describes what happened. "Nurse Desiree came in for her morning shift and checked Sanae's abdominal dressing. Twice a day, the nurses would change the gauze and bandage that covered her open abdomen, mark the bandage with the date, time, and their initials. After checking the date and time, Nurse Desiree lifted the abdominal bandage and then quickly placed it back. She left the room and came back with a surgeon. After the two looked at Sanae's open abdomen, the surgeon quickly left the room and came back with two more surgeons. They all agreed Sanae needed to go to the operating room immediately. An abscess had lodged in her pelvis, and her abdominal cavity was full of infection. They performed an emergency abdominal washout and put her back on the ventilator.

When Linda stepped into the room after she was brought back, she noticed a thick mist or smoke. She asked the nurse what the mist was for, thinking it was yet another machine to perhaps help with her lungs.

> Linda knew that she was seeing something supernatural! It was the Shekinah Glory of God that had filled the room.

With a puzzled look the nurse responded that there was no mist in the room. Linda said, "Yes, I see it; it looks like a smoky mist." The nurse looked around the room and said, "There is no mist or smoke in the room." At that moment Linda knew that she was seeing something supernatural! It was the Shekinah Glory of God that had filled the room. She recognized His presence, the same presence that had shown up in the lounge three days before was now manifested in a magnificent way in the room. Once again, her faith took a giant leap!

For the next five days they kept Sanae on the ventilator and performed two more abdominal cavity washouts. The doctors were concerned about Sanae being intubated for a long period of time and decided that if they weren't able to wean her off the ventilator again, they would perform a tracheotomy. On day 13, Linda signed the papers for the tracheotomy, and once again, she called out for people to pray. On Day 15, they took Sanae down for the tracheotomy. When she returned to her room, she was off the ventilator, and there was no tracheotomy. She was breathing on her own! This was *Miracle number 4!*

At this point, Dr. Nicholas finally acknowledged that Sanae was going to survive. He emphasized that she wasn't out of the woods yet and would have to see him regularly after she was discharged. Linda informed Dr. Nicholas that she and Sanae would be going home to Delaware when discharged. He asked what hospital in Delaware was close to their home, and Linda responded, "Christiana Hospital." He said that he had a colleague at Christiana, and he wanted Sanae to see him. His name is Dr. Tinkoff. Linda looked up Dr. Tinkoff on the internet and called to make an appointment. His receptionist, Rose, informed Linda that Dr. Tinkoff was currently on vacation and not taking new patients. Linda told her about Sanae's condition and that Dr. Nicholas referred them to him. Rose said that she would email Dr. Tinkoff and be back in touch. The very next morning, Rose called and said that Dr. Tinkoff replied immediately and absolutely wanted to see Sanae. It turned out that, by divine providence, Dr. Tinkoff is a top trauma surgeon in the Mid-Atlantic region! This was *Miracle number 5!*

> *Everywhere He rested His nail-pierced hands, He left His blood.*

On Day 20, Sanae was moved down to the sixth floor, the step-down floor for Surgical ICU. On Day 21, the physical therapists had her walking. On Day 27, the surgeons performed skin graft surgery to cover her open abdomen. On Day 33, Sanae was discharged and on her way home to Delaware! What a mighty God we serve!

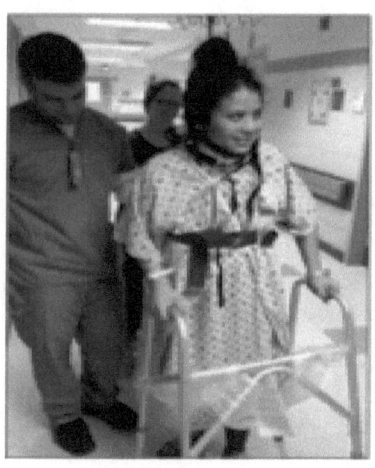

Sanae Walking!

Key Scriptures God Used to Strengthen Linda's Faith:

1. Isaiah 54:13: All your children shall be taught by the Lord, and great shall be the peace of your children.

    Linda's Prayer: *Sanae is taught of the Lord, and great is Sanae's peace and undisturbed composure!*

2. Exodus 23:25: So you shall serve the Lord your God, and He will bless your bread and your water, and I will take sickness away from the midst of you!

Linda's Prayer: *Sanae will serve the Lord, and He will bless her food, and He will take sickness far from her!*

3. Job 33:25–26: His flesh shall be young like a child's, He shall return to the days of his youth. He shall pray to God, and He will delight in him, he shall see His face with joy, for He restores to man His righteousness!

    Linda's Prayer: *Sanae's flesh shall be restored; it is becoming fresher and more tender than a child's. She returns to her youth!*

4. Psalm 30:2: O Lord my God, I cried out to You and You healed me!

    Linda's Prayer: *O Lord my God, I cried out to You, and You have healed Sanae!*

5. Psalm 34:19: Many are the afflictions of the righteous, but the Lord delivers him out of them all!

    Linda's Prayer: *Many evils confront us, but the Lord delivers us out of them all!*

6. Psalm 118:17: I shall not die, but live, and declare the works of the Lord!

    Linda's Prayer: *Sanae will live and not die, and she will declare the works of the Lord and recount the illustrious acts of God!*

7. Matthew 6:33: But seek first the kingdom of God and His righteousness, and all these things shall be added to you!

    Linda's Prayer: *As we seek first the kingdom of God, His righteous, peace, and joy in the Holy Ghost, the abundance within will flow out to every circumstance!*

> *My ability to engage, walk with, listen to, and obey the Holy Spirit is critical to accessing all the abundance that God has prepared and kept ready for me.*

Sonship Principles

Sanae's story models the following sonship principles:

1. Anything the devil is trying to do in my life today cannot be done because of what Jesus already did on the cross 2000 years ago. Jesus's work is finished, lavish, total, and eternal. I cannot be bound, poor, sick, fail, or be oppressed because Jesus has already healed, saved, delivered, and set me free. I am blessed; I cannot be cursed; I am healed; I cannot be sick; I am free; I cannot be bound; I am rich; and I cannot be poor. I cannot be cursed, yoked, or defeated because of what Jesus did for me on the cross. I stand in all the finished works of Christ.

2. My sonship is my key to the supernatural. My ability to engage, walk with, listen to, and obey the Holy Spirit is critical to accessing all the abundance that has been freely given to me by God. This is why Romans 8:14: states, "As many as are led by the spirit of God, they are the sons of God." Understanding and walking in the rights and privileges of sonship requires me to stay connected to God through the Holy Spirit. Sonship means knowing and exercising my spiritual authority. It both requires and enables me to be aware of and engage with God in the spirit. Sonship is my portal to accessing the supernatural and all the provisions that God has prepared and kept ready for me in the spirit.

3. God always hears the cry of the Spirit of His Son! This is a bold cry, a cry of sonship, love, relationship, dependence, trust, expectancy, and reliance. The cry of fear, worry, anxiety, self-pity, powerlessness, and so forth is not the cry of the Spirit of Jesus. It is a strange cry.

4. Sons and daughters of God know their Father. That intimate knowledge of the character of God empowers them to believe God for the miraculous. Daniel 11:32 puts it succinctly. "The people who know their God shall be strong, and do great exploits."

5. When under attack, sons and daughters of God must run to God and hold on! When your heart is breaking, and you feel abandoned by God, run to Him anyway. Tell Him how you feel, pour out your heart, anguish and tears to Him. When you are in this secret place, bruised, battered, prostrate in pain and worship, you are untouchable by the enemy. The Lord will come to your rescue. Psalms 34:18 states that "The Lord is close to the brokenhearted; He rescues those whose spirits are crushed." He will cover you with His wings and shelter you from the storm. He will apply His balm to your wounded heart. He will restore your soul. This is a sacred place, where the enemy cannot follow you in.

6. Sons and daughters of God are not perfect. Being a "son" of God and walking in the rights and privileges of sonship does not require perfection. "Sons" of God are not perfect, but they have a personal relationship with God, are led by the Holy Spirit, and have victory over the flesh, the devil, the world, and sin.

When Sanae awoke from the coma, the Lord spoke to her and said, "You walked a different path than I wanted you to walk, which made you walk away from my protection. But just because you walked away from Me, I never walked away from you. I was there when you got into the accident, but I wouldn't let you die." We are not perfect people, and God is well aware of that. We make bad decisions and wrong choices, but God still loves us and always draws us close.

Gratitude

Linda's summation: "Looking back at our time at Grady Hospital in Atlanta, I want to thank our church family at Word of Life Christian Center in Newark, Delaware.

Our pastors called an emergency prayer meeting the first day of the accident and continued to pray for Sanae throughout her ordeal. After not eating or sleeping for three days, my spiritual daughter, Heather Rivera and her husband Chris, arranged for meals to be delivered to me at the hospital from their home in Texas. Thereafter, Sue Miller from our church took it over and arranged for two meals to be delivered to us every day for the rest of our stay. Our church, friends, and family fed not only me, Debbie, Sanae's Aunt Felicia, and cousin Tabi, but we had enough food to share with other people who had loved ones in the ICU. That was a great testimony of God's love and the love of God's people.

> *You walked away from Me, I never walked away from you.*

Sanae and Linda one month after the accident.

As I read the police report about the collision, I realized two significant things. Remember Sanae's Altima that was totaled four months prior to the accident? If Sanae and her friends had been in that little car at the time of the accident, they would very likely not have survived, as the tractor-trailer would have completely run over that car. God had intervened and protected her four months in advance! The second thing I noticed was the time of the accident and the time that the emergency team arrived at the scene. The EMTs arrived at exactly 2:45 a.m.—the time the Lord woke me in the middle of the night to pray for Sanae.

We are so thankful for Dr. Nicholas, Dr. Tinkoff, all the nurses, medical assistants, and techs at both Grady and Christiana Hospitals. They have all inspired Sanae to change her major and pursue a career in the medical field. Sanae loves to share her story of how great her God is, what He has done for her, and what He will do for others. Whatever you are going through, trust in God. He is faithful and will exceed your expectations with His love, mercy and

> *I don't know how prayer works, but I thank God that it does!*

goodness! As my friend Gloria says, "I don't know how prayer works, but I thank God that it does!" There is a God in heaven who hears us when we pray. And great things happen when sons of God come together in unity and pray according to the will and purpose of God. He is a God who heals, saves, delivers, and restores. He is a God of miracles!" Hallelujah!

Sanae and Linda in 2018

Death of a Child
The Story of Ron Davis Jr.

Thursday March 22, 2012, started out as any other day for the Davis Family. Ron Sr. is a banker and works in New York City. So, as usual, he left home early for his long commute. Vilma is a pediatric nurse practitioner. Taking care of children is her passion. So, after her morning routine, she left for work to do what she loves. Ron and Vilma have been happily married for thirty six years and have built a wonderful family together. They have two amazing children: Ron Jr. and Renee.

Ron Jr. was born in 1983 and Renee in 1987. Ron Sr. and Vilma love Jesus and faithfully taught their children the Word of God. Both Ron Jr. and Renee accepted Christ as their Lord and Savior at a young age. Ron Sr. and Vilma are hands-on parents who are devoted to their children. Despite his long commute to and from work, Ron Sr. made his family a priority. He was there for every game, open house, and Parents Teachers (PTA) meeting. He served on the finance committee of the Brandywine School District as well as the board of the Charter School of Wilmington, when his children attended high school there. He made sure that he and they had a voice in both the school and the school district.

Ron Sr. and Vilma laid a great foundation for their children, not only in faith, home life, and academics, but they also modeled social responsibility for their children. They are members of Premiere Charities, a local organization that serves the homeless in downtown Wilmington. Every other Sunday, the Davis family volunteered and served food to the less fortunate. In addition, Ron Sr. and Vilma are Christian ministers and serve in their local church. In 2010, Vilma founded MPUSH (Mothers Praying Until Something

Happens). This is a ministry that empowers women to be on the offensive in consistently praying for their children, as well as children in their neighborhood, community, and the nation. Vilma explains, "I believe children are a blessing, a gift, from God, and as such we need to protect our blessing."

The Davis Family – the early years.

Ron Jr.

Like his parents, Ron Jr. loved to help others. At Premiere Charities, he not only served food to the homeless, he was the go-to man for video montages. He worked endless hours to make sure that each video perfectly reflected the person who was being honored. In addition, he also volunteered to help kids at the Al Dupont hospital. In short, Ron Jr. was an editor, tutor, handyman, driver, and simply an extra hand to anyone in need. Ron Sr. recalls fondly, "When Ron Jr. was at New York University, he visited Ghana. He bought school supplies and other gifts with his own money to give to the students in Ghana."

Ron Jr. Graduates from NYU.

Ron Jr's love for helping others was paralleled only by his love for sports. He loved all things sports! He was six feet, three inches tall and loved to play football and basketball. He was passionate about sports

Ron Jr. is every parent's dream child!

and loved all the New York teams. From the Mets to the Knicks to the Giants, Ron cheered for them all! He was over the moon when the New York Giants, barely making it to the playoffs, went on to be the Super Bowl champions.

Ron Jr. is every parent's dream child! Growing up, he was a straight A student and consistently on the honor roll. He was a Boy Scout and earned the highly coveted Eagle award; the highest rank for the Boy Scout. He attended high school at the Charter School of Wilmington and went on to attend New York University in Manhattan, New York, where he graduated cum laude from the

Gallatin School of Individualized Studies after three and a half years. After graduation, he moved to Los Angeles, California, to pursue a career in script writing but ended up working for Raymond James. After a couple of years, he returned to Wilmington, Delaware, and went to work at the former Mellon Bank in Philadelphia. A couple months later, the Mellon Bank merged with the Bank of New York where his father worked. In 2010, Ron Jr. was transferred to the Bank's Delaware office where he worked as an assistant portfolio officer.

Renee Davis is also an outstanding and accomplished young woman. Growing up, she looked up to her big brother and wanted to emulate him in every way. He was a straight A student, so Renee had to be a straight A student. He was a Boy Scout, and she was a Girl Scout. He got his Eagle award, and she got her Gold award. She wanted to follow in her big brother's footsteps. Renee explains: "He was an amazing big brother, always looking out for me and protecting me. We had this awesome friendship. When I was in college in DC, I called him a lot and asked for advice. When he moved to California, I visited him there, and he took such good care of me! When he bought his home in Wilmington, I would go over and hang out with him. He was always there for me."

In 2012, Ron Jr. was on an upward trajectory, and things were looking up. He had decided to go to graduate school and was accepted into the Darden School of Business at the University of Virginia with a full scholarship. He also had just started seriously dating a beautiful young woman who made his heart smile. At the same time, Renee was pursuing a doctorate degree in psychology. Today, she works in Maryland, providing therapy to children and adolescents.

The Davis family is by all accounts, a very blessed, accomplished, respectable, and respected Christian family. Then tragedy struck!

The Unthinkable Happens

It was after 5 p.m. on March 22, 2012, and the end of a very busy day. For Vilma, it was time to go home. Except for one of her colleagues, everyone else had already left for the day. She picked up her pocketbook and checked her phone to see if she had any calls, texts, or emails. Surprisingly, there was a voice message from Ron Jr's manager. As she listened, so many turbulent emotions swept over her. She was anxious, confused, and somewhat bewildered. The message simply said "Mrs. Davis, it is important that you call me as soon as possible."

Davis Family - From right to left: Ron Sr., Vilma's uncle, Rev. Clement Gayle, Ron Jr., Renee, Vilma (Sitting Down)

This message changed Vilma's life forever! Her heart began to pound. Why did the manager from her son's office call to speak to her? Why was there such an urgency in his voice? She looked at

> *Vilma's intuition told her something was horribly wrong.*

her watch. It was 5:30 p.m. She realized that most offices were probably already closed for the day But she felt the need to return that call. So, she did. As she expected, her call went to voice mail. So, she decided to call her son; that call also went to voicemail.

Vilma's intuition told her something was horribly wrong. She started to shake. By this time, she was standing beside her car in the parking garage. She thought, "Maybe Ron Jr. had gone to work and became sick at the office or was in some sort of accident." Her office was located on the premises of a hospital, so she decided to walk over to the emergency room area to look around. "Can I help you?" a voice asked. "Do you have a patient admitted here by the name of Ronald Davis?" Vilma asked. What followed was a moment's silence, which seemed liked hours. Then the voice came back: "No, ma'am, there is no record of a Ronald Davis," Vilma walked back to her car and started to cry. She called her sister and told her that Ron's boss had left her an urgent voice mail. She asked her sister to call a couple other hospitals to see if Ron Jr. was admitted there.

Ron Jr's condominium was less than ten minutes away, so Vilma decided to go over to see if he was there. Vilma describes what happens next: "As I reached the entrance to the complex, my feet felt very heavy as if they were weighted down and dragging. It felt as if I was walking in mud. I went up to the desk and said, 'I am here to see Ron Davis.' As the words came out of my mouth, I started to shake uncontrollably, the doorman said to me, 'Oh, didn't you hear? He passed away this morning.' 'He what!' I screamed as I collapsed in a heap on the floor. 'He passed away this morning," the doorman repeated. After some phone calls by my colleague, he found out where my son's body was and took me over to the coroner's office. There, laying on a table was my twenty eight year old son's body. I prayed for God to raise him up from the dead, but nothing happened."

Vilma was utterly devastated! She called Ron Sr. who was on the bus coming back from New York and asked him to get home right away! She was in total disbelief! Just the night before, her only son and firstborn child had visited with her at home. He had come over as he usually does for leftovers. He ate, and they talked for a while. After his father came home from work, Vilma left them together to watch the basketball game on TV, while she went to her room to write a post for her blog "Empowering Mothers." At about 10 p.m., she heard his voice call out "Hey, Mom, I'm leaving." She came to the top of the stairs to say goodnight, "Okay, son, see you tomorrow." She said. She had no inkling that this would be the last time she would see him alive.

The unthinkable has happened, and the Davis family was heartbroken and reeling from this devastation! They were in uncharted territory. There were no reference manuals for this catastrophe, and they did not know what to do. Suddenly, their world had collapsed around them, sending them into a deep, dark valley. It felt so unreal; all these people coming over and expressing sympathy. They were planning a funeral instead of a wedding, picking out a casket instead of a tuxedo. Instead of seeing their son off to graduate school where he was awarded a full scholarship, they were taking him to the cemetery for burial. They were stunned, perplexed, and immobilized!

Ron Jr.

Questions were swirling around their heads. What does one do when, without any warning, your child goes to bed never to wake up on this earth again? How do you explain this tragedy of losing a well-behaved son, born again Christian, well educated, employed in a great job, and living a life pleasing to God? What answers do you have to explain why a twenty eight year old young man, who was never out on the streets, was always working out in the gym, had so many goals and aspirations, was three weeks into a love relationship, and getting ready to go to graduate school, would suddenly pass away with no warning. How does a Christian family ministering to so many people, continue life without losing their faith or being consumed by bitterness and anger? God how could you do this to us? Why God, why?

Journey Through the Valley

The next couple of weeks were very difficult. Vilma explains "After the funeral was over, I truly felt empty. I did not cry during the entire funeral service because I couldn't cry. The tears never flowed outwardly, but I was flooded on the inside. A couple days after the funeral, the tears started to flow again. My heart felt as if it was broken into many little pieces. I was so sad. The coroner's report was that our son had an enlarged heart, which caused his death. As a pediatric nurse practitioner, I started to blame myself; I went over and over in my mind what I may have missed. After being at home for about two weeks, I returned to work, I truly needed to be distracted from those overpowering thoughts in my mind. My husband returned to work after about one week, and our daughter went back to Washington, DC. It was very difficult to go back to my son's condo and pack it up. Although some people volunteered to help, my husband and I decided to pack his things by ourselves. Somehow, I felt that I did not want anyone else to touch his things. We cried through the entire ordeal and took many breaks until we eventually got the job completed."

In her book, *On Death and Dying*, Elizabeth Kubler Ross discusses five emotional stages that a person potentially goes through when facing impending death or the loss of a loved one. Ross's book has helped countless people make sense of the feelings that they experience after a painful loss. The five stages are chronologically: denial, anger, bargaining, depression, and acceptance.

In her book, Ross explains that denial is a common defense mechanism that buffers the immediate shock of the loss, numbing us to our emotions. As the masking effects of denial and isolation begin to wear, reality and its pain re-emerge. But, we are not ready. So, the intense emotion is deflected from our vulnerable core, redirected, and expressed instead as anger. Anger may be directed at our deceased loved one. Even though, rationally, we know the person is not to blame, emotionally, however, we may resent the person for causing us pain or for leaving us. We feel guilty for being angry, and this makes us angrier. At the bargaining stage, we often have a feeling of guilt. This is the period where we go through a series of "If only" statements. We start to believe there was something we could have done differently to have helped save our loved one. Depression is the fourth stage of grief. There are two types of depression that are associated with mourning. The first is a reaction to the practical implications of the loss. Sadness and regret predominate this type of depression. The second type of depression is subtler and, in a sense, perhaps more private. It is our quiet preparation to separate and to bid our loved one farewell. Sometimes all we really need is a hug. The fifth and final stage of grief is described by Kubler-Ross as acceptance. This phase is marked by withdrawal and calm. Getting to this stage of grieving is a gift not afforded to everyone. Some individuals may never go beyond anger or denial.

Coping with loss is ultimately a deeply personal and individual experience. Nobody can help you go through it more easily or understand all the emotions you are experiencing. But others can be there for you and help comfort you through this process. The best thing to do is to allow yourself to feel the grief as it comes over you. Resisting it will only prolong the natural process of healing.

Vilma explains her journey through the five stages of grief: "I went back and forth between the stages of denial and anger for a while. I found it difficult to believe that my son who never exhibited any signs of a heart condition, who had such dreams and aspirations, was snatched from us without warning. It couldn't be. Of course, we are a Christian family, we love the Lord, we loved others, I ministered to mothers, empowering them to pray for their children consistently and telling them that their children were gifts from God. Why me, why our only son, why not take our house, car, why not take me, instead of my son? During my fits of anger and denial, I still cried out to the Lord in prayer. Each time I blurted out a question in my anguish, He would respond with "I love you, I loved your son, and the love I have for him far surpasses the love you have for him." I knew that this was true, but my heart was too wounded to trust. To get this truth from my head to my heart, I had to keep repeating it over and over. I would sing for hours— "Jesus loves me this I know, for the Bible tells me so." After sometime I got it. A God who loves us so much, would not do anything to hurt us.

Lessons Learned in the Valley

During this time, God taught the Davis family many life lessons. Here are some of them:

1. Ron Jr. was not just a gift from God, but a gift *on loan* from God. That means that God had the right to call him home at any time. This revelation impacted Vilma's ministry to mothers. For the Davis family, their mess became their message. They redefined their ministry vision and mission to include the statement that "children are a gift on loan from God." This revelation also birthed a new ministry—the Turning Point Ministry which today, is transforming people's lives by pointing them to the love of God.

2. Seek professional counseling help. Losing a child is a major trauma, and it can destroy lives and marriages. Just like you go to get help for a physical trauma like an auto accident, you should seek professional help for the emotional trauma of losing a child.

Continue to minister to others even in your pain.

3. Continue to minister to others even in your pain. The Davis Family continued with their MPUSH ministry and launched a new Turning Point ministry to help others navigate and deal with emotional pain. The devil tried to stop these ministries. He attacked Vilma's mind with negative thoughts like, "You are helping others; who is helping you?" But she persevered and refused to be deterred.

4. Keep moving forward! The devil wants to stop you in your tracks. He wants to make this tragedy the last story of your life. But don't let the devil win! Our God can bring life out of death. The victory of God transcends your pain. He is the Lord over every circumstance and situation. Keep walking. Keep putting one foot in front of another. And you are coming out! The Lord is taking you through and out of the valley.

5. The God of the mountain is still God in the valley. Run to God in your pain. Go to Him with your questions, anger, and tears. Rely on God and His Word. Be real and honest with God. The saying that "Real men don't cry" is a lie. Jesus was a real man and He wept.

Things Not to Say to Grieving Parents

Most people mean well. They feel sorrow for grieving parents and want to help. However, in their effort to find words of comfort, they may say things that can hurt more that help. Here are some things *not* to say to a parent who has lost a child:

1. You have other children or you are young, so you can have another child. Even if this is true, another child is not a substitute for the child that was lost. Each child is unique and

> *A God who loves us so much, would not do anything to hurt us.*

2. special. The loss of an individual child is a devastating loss and cannot be made up by another child.

3. I lost my mother, sister, father, friend, and so on. These losses, while equally painful, are not the same as losing a child. When we lose a parent, we lose our past; when we lose a sibling, we lose the present; but when you lose a child, you lose the future. Unless you have experienced the pain of losing a child, do not compare your loss with theirs.

3. You need to get over it. It is true that some grieving can be unhealthy; however, it's not that simple. Unless you have a practical and proven solution to enable that person to move forward, keep quiet. Maybe they would have moved on if they knew how to.

4. Don't say, "I know what you are going through" because you probably don't. Even if you have lost a child, the circumstances surrounding the loss will likely be different and so will the pain and hurt.

5. Don't say "He is in a better place." Even though that is true for Christians, it is little comfort to the grieving parent. As far as they are concerned, the best place for the child to be is alive, with them.

The good news is you don't have to say anything; just be there. Your presence and silent support mean much more than groping for and saying the wrong things. A good rule of thumb is, if you do not know what to say, a hug and "I love you" speaks volumes and is enough.

Also, you can send a card, especially around the holidays to say, "Thinking about you."

> *Your presence and silent support mean much more than groping for words and saying the wrong things.*

A New Normal

Things do not go back to normal after the burial. In fact, they will never go back to normal because the old normal is gone forever. You have to find a new normal. Although the phone calls and visits stop as people go back to their own lives, the grieving family still wrestles with coming to terms with the loss, picking up the pieces, establishing a new normal, and moving forward. Birthdays, holidays, Mother's Day, and Father's Day are especially hard. Also, getting an invitation to a wedding, a baby's dedication, or a graduation from your child's peers can trigger memories and grief because it is a reminder of the future that was stolen by death.

Grieving families may struggle with feeling violated in a very deep way and robbed. They may resent the loss and feel that it was unfair. There may also be a very strong sense of helplessness, vulnerability, and fear. If not addressed, these feelings can keep you from healing and finding a new normal. Bring them to God. Only He can heal and restore your soul.

There are practical situations that may challenge your quest for a new normal. For example, you may run into people who ask innocently, "How many children do you have?" or "Do you have a sibling?" How do you answer these questions? For the Davis family, do they say one child? Would that be betraying the memory of Ron Jr.? What if they answered, "We have two children," and then the questioner probes further? These, questions and their answers can reopen old wounds and cause pain. In these situations, your willingness to answer and how much you say depends on who is asking the question, how close the relationship is, how you are feeling at the moment, and how much time you have to talk. Whatever you do, don't allow yourself to be dragged back into the past.

Sometimes, a physical activity or new routine could be helpful in establishing a new normal. For Renee, kickboxing became an outlet for some of her anger. Ron Jr's death has changed her life forever. She is now effectively an only child. She stays close to her parents and checks in with them regularly. When they call her in the morning, she makes sure to answer the phone, so they'll know that she is okay. When she feels angry and frustrated about the loss, she goes kickboxing and makes the devil pay!

Establishing a new normal is different for each family. God is a very present help in time of grief. Rest in Him and trust His love. It is imperative that the love of God is constantly communicated, not just by words but actions. Ask yourself, how can I use this tragic event for good? How can God be glorified? How do you prevent Satan from getting victory? As you ponder these questions and seek God for answers, you will realize that God is at work, and healing is taking place.

Key Scriptures God Used to Strengthen the Davis Family:

1. Job 13:15 (KJV): Though he slay me, yet will I trust in him: but I will maintain mine own ways before him.

2. Psalms 23:4 (KJV): Yea, though I walk through the valley of the shadow of death, I will fear no evil: for thou art with me; thy rod and thy staff they comfort me.

3. Isaiah 43:2 (KJV): When thou passest through the waters, I will be with thee; and through the rivers, they shall not overflow thee: when thou walkest through the fire, thou shalt not be burned; neither shall the flame kindle upon thee.

4. Job 19:25 (KJV): For I know that my redeemer liveth, and that he shall stand at the latter day upon the earth.

Vilma explains how the Word of God helped her: "Though I am wobbly, I believe every word of every one of these verses. I know that I am not alone! I have a great big, wonderful God who is with me. I do not pretend to understand all that is happening at the moment, but I know that God will be glorified."

Sonship Principles

The Davis family story models the following sonship principles:

1. Fatherhood is a central and dominant theme in the Bible. The reason is simple. God is a Father! In scripture, there are many different names used to describe God. While all the names of God are significant and very important in their meaning and revelation of the character of God, the name, Abba Father, is perhaps the most tender of all because it identifies the special,

> *I am not alone! I have a great, big, wonderful, God who is with me.*

close, intimate relationship of a father and his beloved child. Jesus taught us to call God "Abba Father" or Daddy.

2. The Holy Spirit brings God's fatherly love to us and brings our childlike affections for God. This is the Spirit of adoption making real to us the love of our Father, applying it to us so that we know that we are loved. He makes the truth of our acceptance and the value of our Father real to us and pours out the love of the Father into our lives (Romans 5:5). We *enjoy* emotionally the Fatherhood of God by the testimony of the Spirit (John Piper).

3. For sons and daughters of God, the Bible is the infallible Word of God and the final authority on all questions, issues, and discussions. When life doesn't make sense and they cannot explain their circumstances, sons of God cling to the Word of God. They trust the nature and character of God.

4. When under attack, sons and daughters of God must run to God and hold on! When your heart is breaking, and you feel abandoned by God, run to Him anyway. Tell Him how you feel, pour out your heart, anguish and tears to Him. When you are in this secret place, bruised, battered, prostrate in pain and worship, you are untouchable by the enemy. The Lord will come to your rescue. Psalms 34:18 (NLT) states that "The Lord is close to the brokenhearted; He rescues those whose spirits are crushed." He will cover you with His wings and shelter you from the storm. He will apply His balm to your wounded heart. He will restore your soul. This is a sacred place, where the enemy cannot follow you in.

> *When Jesus was crucified, God also lost (gave) His only son.*

> *When under attack, sons and daughters of God must run to God and hold on!*

5. Sons and daughters of God are willing to partake in the fellowship of Christ's suffering. In Philippians 3:8-11, apostle Paul makes it personal when he declared:

> Yes, everything else is worthless when compared with the infinite value of knowing Christ Jesus my Lord. For his sake I have discarded everything else, counting it all as garbage, so that I could gain Christ and become one with him. . . . For God's way of making us right with himself depends on faith. I want to know Christ and experience the mighty power that raised him from the dead. I want to suffer with him, sharing in his death, so that one way or another I will experience the resurrection from the dead!

The Davis family has established a new normal. They have drawn strength from the Word of God to move forward. They have chosen to trust God no matter what! They know that God is good all the time and is involved even in the dark details of our lives. There is a balm in Gilead. His name is Jesus. He is our high priest who is able to empathize and sympathize with us in life's darkest valleys because He has been there Himself. The Davis family are experiencing the power of God to heal broken hearts. They know that when the devil does his worst, our God is bigger, stronger, mightier, and more powerful. The story of the Davis family is still being written. God still has the pen, and when it's all over, He will bring beauty out of these ashes.

> *When the devil does his worst, our God is bigger, stronger, mightier, and more powerful.*

Our Identity in Christ
The Story of Vivalyn Elvy

Vivalyn Elvy is a beautiful woman, wife, mother, author, business woman, and minister. She has a bachelor's degree in liberal arts and a master's in business administration. Vivalyn was born in Jamaica, West Indies. She immigrated to the United States when she was twelve years old to live with her father in New York. Throughout her youth, she heard family members say to her, "Your nose is *so* big" or "Your hair is *so* bad. After hearing those words repeatedly over the years, Vivalyn felt unattractive and developed a sense of inferiority. In her teen years, this inferiority complex played a big role in how she perceived herself. She had very low self-esteem and did not believe or see herself as beautiful.

Meet Vivalyn

While driving home late one night, Vivalyn began to cry out to God. She told the Lord the lies that she had been led to believe about herself, that she was ugly and that no one would ever want her. God interrupted her tears with His response! What He said shocked her!

The Lord said to her so clearly, "You are calling Me a liar." She promptly replied "No way, *God.* I would never call You a liar." Then God said, "Didn't I say that everything I have made is good and that you are fearfully and wonderfully made? So, when you call yourself ugly, you are calling Me a liar."

This encounter with God was a turning point in Vivalyn's life and began a process of transformation in her thinking. The Bible says in Proverbs 23:7 that "As a man thinks in his heart, so is he." Vivalyn realized that to change her life, she needed to change her thinking. The change process culminated in a journey of self-discovery.

Journey of Self Discovery

Over the years, as she grew in her walk with God, Vivalyn's encounter with the Lord blossomed into a journey of self-discovery. Vivalyn says: "The first thing I discovered on my journey was that I needed to learn how to get rid of my negative thoughts toward myself, my marriage, my past, and so on and allow God's Word to transform my mind. I had to let God step in and redefine my thoughts about myself.

You see, like you and many others, I had allowed society, friends, and family to define who I am, and many of you, like me, can testify to the damage this may have caused. But I am so thankful to God that He will never give up on us. He will cause His truths to revolutionize the way we see ourselves if we allow Him to. He cancels every lie with *His* truth, which I found to be liberating, kind, loving, and outright powerful."

Another thing Vivalyn discovered on her journey was that the words we speak to ourselves, our children, grandchildren, friends, and

> *Our words are a powerful force; it can change and rearrange things.*

family can affect future generations. Per Vivalyn, "Our words are a powerful force; it can change and rearrange things. Therefore, it is vitally important for us to think before we speak. Proverbs 18:20–21 says, "A man's [moral] self shall be filled with the fruit of his mouth; and with the consequence of his words he must be satisfied [whether good or evil]. Death and life are in the power of the tongue, and they who indulge in it shall eat the fruit of it [death or life]" (emphasis added). In other words, our words have power, and they can either produce life or death!

Today, Vivalyn is a beautiful woman who is filled with the spirit of God and a firm understanding of His love for her. She has written a book, "*Who Am I*," to help other people struggling with their body image and identity issues. *Who Am I* chronicles Vivalyn's journey of self-discovery and offers a pathway to wholeness in Christ. Vivalyn says: "We are all faced with this question one time or another in our lives. Everywhere we go, we are being told who we are, whether it's by the media, scientists, society, our friends, or families. They all have an opinion as to who we are, and I have experienced and seen the negative effects their words can have. I have taken a journey of self-discovery, and I invite everyone to take their own journey and to see themselves through the eyes of a loving Father who wants more for them than they want for themselves.

> *God cancels every lie with His truth!*

"*Who Am I*" challenges the status quo. It is a call to introspection, self-examination and re-definition. *Who Am I* calls us to account based on the Word of God and says "it is time"—time for us to *stop* believing the lies we have heard from our family, friends, society, and even ourselves, and put on God's truths about our authentic identity, the identity that is found in Christ Jesus. When it all comes down to it, God *is* love, and that's all we must accept: His love for us. God has never been disappointed with us, why? Because He only sees us the way we truly are, in Christ. The blood of Christ has covered *all* our past, present, and future sins and therefore, the Father only sees us as completed, whole, and perfected. We may have been confused as to who we are, but He is not and never will be."

Thus, it is vitally important to renew our minds with the Word of God so we can think about ourselves the way God thinks about us. This is because our thoughts become *our words*, our words will then *affect* our *emotions* and our *actions*, and then our emotions and actions (good or bad) will become *our way of life*. So, it is imperative that we guard our hearts and minds from toxic thoughts and words and allow God's Word to transform our thoughts and our words.

Key Scriptures God Used to Transform Vivalyn

1. First was the Scripture that God spoke to her that fateful night—Psalm 139:14. As Vivalyn pondered this scripture, the Holy Spirit opened her heart and mind to her true value as a "son" of God.

Vivalyn explains the revelation that she received: "God said that we are fearfully and wonderfully made. He made us in His image and in

> *God has never been disappointed with us, because He only sees us the way we truly are, in Christ.*

His likeness. He calls us His inheritance and says that we are holy, righteous, and valuable enough for Him to die for us! He says that we are His children, His mansion, light and salt of the world, and that we are His incredible work of art."

This understanding, from the Word of God, of her personal value contrasted heavily with what Vivalyn had been told by relatives and in science class at school. She had been told by society and scientists that we are just humans, evolved from apes, and that there is nothing significant about us. Other than our highly developed brains, there is no purpose for our existence, and we have no value or importance. We are just here to live, work, reproduce, and die.

> *What you believe about God does not define who God is, but what God says about you does define who you are.*

But that is all a lie. The truth is that we are of inestimable value. Our value comes from our source, God Himself. Our value does not come from our performance, whether or not people like us, how much money we have, our net worth, who we know, what we drive, how we look, and so forth. God is our source of origin, and that source will never diminish in value. Vivalyn realized that she had bought into a lie and that her value does not come from her looks, the shape or size of her nose, or the texture of her hair. She further realized that the voices that told her that she was not good enough were unqualified to make that assessment. God, her Source and Maker, is the only person qualified to speak on this subject, and He says that she is fearfully and wonderfully made!

That day, Vivalyn discovered what we all need to know and believe: "it doesn't matter what we think or what society, friends, or our family says or thinks about us. What matters most is *what* God believes and says about us. You see, what you believe about God does not define who God is, but what God says about you *does* define who you are."

2. Another Scripture that God used to transform Vivalyn was Galatians 3:26–28. It states:

> For in Christ Jesus you are all sons of God through faith. For as many [of you] as were baptized into Christ [into a spiritual union and communion with Christ, the Anointed One, the Messiah] have put on (clothed yourselves with) Christ. There is [now no distinction] neither Jew nor Greek, there is neither slave nor free, there is not male and female; for you are all one in Christ Jesus.

As a result, your identity is found in Christ. The Holy Spirit taught Vivalyn that to be "in Christ" means that you have accepted His sacrifice on the cross as payment for your sins and turned from your evil ways to live as and for Christ. Your rap sheet containing every sinful thought, attitude, or action has been wiped clean once you place your faith in Jesus Christ. You have been made whole, righteous, perfect, justified, and *complete* in Him. Your old identity is gone! You have a new identity; it is found in Christ.

Sonship Principles

Vivalyn's story models the following sonship principles:

1. God has placed tremendous value in us—He calls us sons and daughters! I am a son/daughter of God. I am an heir of God and a joint heir with Christ. Jesus gave His life for me—

that defines my value as a son of God. I must recognize my personal value and own it.

2. Self-talk is very important because it outlines the image of myself that I have on the inside. My self-image is critical because what I believe and say about myself has the greatest impact on my life more than any other person's words spoken over me.

3. Simply stated, the Word of God coming out of my mouth, in faith, is the most potent weapon known to man. What this means, is that every word I speak is on assignment. Once I believe the Word in my heart and launch it forth via the spoken word, it will not return empty; it will achieve its creative purpose and assignment. It is unstoppable!

Sons and daughters of God have tremendous value. Recognizing the immeasurable value God placed on her life and seeing herself through the eyes of God set Vivalyn free from decades of low self-esteem and the lies of the devil. Many teenagers have committed suicide because of a negative self-image and harmful words spoken over them by friends and relatives. Today, Vivalyn is a wife, mother of two, and an author. She has devoted herself to teaching and empowering others to break free from the bondage of low self-esteem. Her book *Who Am I* is eloquent testimony of the grace and faithfulness of God to heal and deliver. It challenges readers to believe that if God did it for Vivalyn, He can do it for them, too.

Broken, Restored, and Hopeful
The Story of Erin Kline

Have you every struggled with disagreeing with someone's lifestyle or decisions but are not sure how to tell them? Have you ever found yourself in a situation where people were bashing God or making fun of godly principles, and you were the only Christian there? Have you ever had to stand up for what you felt was right or had to say no at the risk of losing a relationship, job, or great opportunity? Have you ever found yourself in a compromising location or situation due to circumstances beyond your control? Have you ever walked away from "the love of your life" because you felt, deep within, that he was not God's will for you? If you answered yes to any of these questions, you can relate to the story of Erin Kline.

Erin is a beautiful and charming young woman with a heart of gold. She is a special education teacher. She has a bachelor's degree in deaf studies and a master's degree in early intervention with infants who are deaf-blind. She works with infants and children who are deaf-blind and their families. Erin is also a Christian minister. She leads REACH—a community outreach ministry that provides services to the poor, homeless, senior citizens, and people who are shut in, and performs random acts of kindness.

Erin's Sister

Erin has an identical twin sister, and they are very close! Aside from bonding for nine months in the womb, they grew up in a very rural area with few kids, so they were pretty much all each other had. Growing up, Erin was the girly girl, and her sister was more of a tomboy. Erin would play GI Joes and basketball with her, and she would play house and school with Erin. Even though their interests and personalities were totally opposite, their bond as twin sisters, couldn't have been stronger. Erin explains "She was my four-minute 'older sister,' and she certainly took on that role, continually protecting me and looking out for me. I always looked up to her and was her biggest cheerleader."

Early on in their high school years, her sister confided in Erin that she was attracted to girls. Erin loved, supported, encouraged, and advocated for her. She thought that this was who she was, something she was born with, and nothing she could change. She came out to their family in her senior year in high school. Their mom accepted her homosexual lifestyle and grew to support and encourage it, but their dad and several other family members opposed it, which led to extreme hurt, distance, and a separation in the family for several years.

Erin and her sister

Erin and Jesus

When Erin was nineteen years old, in her second year of college, she became a born again Christian. Her life changed drastically! Almost instantly, she encountered opposition, especially from her mom, who asked, "So, now that you're saved, do you think your sister is going to hell because she's gay?" Over the next nine years, Erin grew in her faith, but she had learned early on to be quiet about her faith around her family and friends, so she said nothing. Erin was a people pleaser and did not want to disrupt the status quo. She explains: "Growing up, I did what everyone wanted and expected me to do. I wanted to be liked, I wanted to fit in, I wanted to be a peacemaker, and I wanted to make everybody happy.

Erin and her sister/best friend

My pastor once said, 'Those who lack identity will take on the identity of those around them,' and I did just that. I was a different person, depending on who I was around. I did not have any healthy boundaries. I avoided saying no for fear of

> *Those who lack identity will take on the identity of those around them.*

hurting those close to me and to keep them happy. I was a people-pleaser, especially when it came to my family. I just wanted them to feel loved and to love me in return."

In 2011, her sister, who had been dating her girlfriend for almost nine years, told Erin that she was seriously considering proposing. Just like any sister, she wanted Erin's thoughts on how to propose, ideas on the ring, and her overall support. In February of 2011, she proposed, her girlfriend accepted, and the wedding planning began. While Erin wanted to celebrate and jump for joy with her, she felt conflicted because of her relationship with God and what she really believed about homosexuality and the definition of marriage. Erin knew the time had come for her to speak up. She was terrified! An internal struggle was raging within her. On the one hand, she loved God and wanted to put Him first and obey Him, but on the other hand, she loved her sister and wanted to be everything her sister wanted, needed, and deserved. She felt like she was being pulled apart by this internal tug of war.

> *How could she put God first at the risk of shattering her sister?*

She knew that as a Christian, she would be living a lie by not speaking up, but at the same time, she felt that she would be betraying her sister if she did. She kept wondering, what if God told her not to be maid of honor at her sister's wedding because doing so would be like agreeing with same-sex marriage—or what if God led her to not attend the wedding altogether? How could she put God first at the risk of shattering her sister? What would happen if she really stood up for what she believed, knowing she'd be standing up for God but against her family and most importantly, her best friend?

Broken

On Memorial Day 2011, things came to a head. Erin had made up her mind. She had made the decision to honor God and to risk losing her relationship with her sister. Her sister and her fiancée had a cookout at their house. Erin, her mom, and stepdad attended. As everyone was eating and relaxing, they started talking about the upcoming wedding. Because this had been weighing so heavily on her heart, Erin began to cry, and it all came spilling out.

She told her sister that she loved her and her fiancée, but when it came to their marriage, she didn't think that same-sex marriage was God's plan. She explained that it wasn't that she was disgusted by them being together, no longer liked her fiancée, or had suddenly become homophobic. She still loved them just as much as she always had. It was simply the truth of God's Word. She then told her sister that she wanted to really pray about the wedding and her role in it because for the first time in her life, it was her heart's desire to put God first.

> *This was the hardest thing I've ever had to do, but God's love and grace showed up strong.*

Erin describes what happened next "It was like I zapped the life right out of my sister, and the hurt was so evident. Because of our unique connection, I knew exactly what she was feeling. She felt alone and betrayed by her best friend. The one constant in her life was now telling her that she didn't agree with her lifestyle and the rights and approval she so desperately wanted. The hurt, tension, anger, and pain were more real than anything any of us had ever felt. My mom accused me of being judgmental, and the cookout was brought to a screeching halt. By this time, my sister and I were both in tears. I decided to leave. As I left, my mom was silent and distant. My sister and I hugged, both agreeing that somehow, we would get through this. This was by far, the hardest thing I've ever had to do, but God's love and grace showed up strong. That day, I made the personal decision that I didn't want anything or anyone to come between me and God and His plan for my life."

Process

"The months following were terrible. I desperately wanted things to go back to normal, but I had spoken those words of truth, and they couldn't be taken back. Though it felt like the greatest loss I'd ever experienced, I hoped and trusted that God was working to make it the greatest gain I would ever experience! He placed an incredible man of God, who was my boyfriend at the time, and some of the greatest friends and support system in my life that He knew I would need to get through this tough time. Even though that day will always be remembered with some of the worst pain I've ever felt, the rush of relief I experienced after I put God first was also unlike any weight that had ever been lifted off my shoulders. On that day, I understood what Jesus meant when He said that you will know the truth, and the truth will set you free. I didn't know what to expect after that day, but God's grace, His truth, and His presence in my life changed me."

Over the next couple of months, Erin's relationship with her mom and sister was very strained. Intermittently, they would each send her articles claiming biblical evidence in support of homosexuality and how being homosexual is something that you're born with and irrevocable. Her sister would compare it to the color of her skin, saying that it was nothing she could change. She asked Erin why she would have voluntarily chosen this lifestyle, given the rejection, the looks of disapproval and the societal prejudices. Erin's mom went days without talking to her, and when they finally talked, it seemed like the fakest and quickest conversations ever. Over time, Erin built a lot of resentment toward her mom because she felt that her mom went above and beyond to support her sister's lifestyle, and in the process, put Erin down and disrespected her beliefs. Erin and her sister were so frustrated, sad, and mad and just wanted desperately for things to go back to how they were before, but they didn't know how to fix it.

The months leading up to the wedding were filled with intense emotion, confusion, and feelings of betrayal; but underlying everything, was the indescribable relationship that God had formed between Erin and her sister. After expressing her true beliefs, Erin felt released by God to love her sister and her fiancée by being in their wedding. So, Erin was her maid of honor and helped to make the wedding the most special event in her life.

Erin as maid of honor for her sister.

Erin shares a quote by Rick Warren that made a big impact on her and helped her through this time: "Our culture has accepted two huge lies. The first is that if you disagree with someone's lifestyle, you must fear or hate them. The second is that to love someone means you agree with everything they believe or do. Both are nonsense. You don't have to compromise convictions to be compassionate." This quote hit home for Erin and validated so much for her. She learned that she could love her sister without accepting or condoning her lifestyle. She also learned that speaking the truth in a loving way that shows genuine care and grace is not being judgmental and is, in fact, the only way to be effective as a Christian.

Restored!

Now, almost seven years later, Erin can honestly say that her relationship with her sister is closer than it's ever been. It is such a glorious testimony of God's love, grace, and mercy. They still butt heads when the topic of homosexuality and Christianity is brought up, but at the same time, they are the closest of friends. God has also worked to heal Erin's relationship with her mom.

During the confrontation with her sister, God had placed a wonderful man of God in Erin's life: her boyfriend at the time. He was an amazing guy! First and foremost, he was a strong and faithful Christian. He was involved in his church, spent time daily studying the Word of God and in prayer. He truly sought to live out His Christian faith to bring others closer to the Lord. In addition, he was financially stable, in a career he enjoyed, was a people person, very charismatic, great with Erin's family, close with his own family, had an incredible sense of humor that made Erin laugh constantly, and was the most romantic, creative, and thoughtful guy ever. He was all around everything a girl could ever want or ask for.

Erin and her sister/best friend

Erin's Boyfriend

He swept Erin off her feet! Her family loved him, and everybody including Erin thought that she had finally met "the one." In the three years they were together, they talked about the rest of their lives, looked at engagement rings, and planned for the future. Despite all of that, deep within, something nagged at Erin from early on. She felt that something wasn't quite right, but she kept pushing the feeling aside because on paper, everything looked great. She couldn't have asked for more. As with any relationship, there were a few things that they struggled with but nothing they couldn't work through, or so they thought. When small things kept popping up, they went to counseling to find the root of the problem and work through it. Over time, these small things became bigger stumbling blocks. The arguments began, and they seemed to hit a brick wall every time. Try as much as they could, they couldn't work through these issues, even though they both desperately wanted to.

Broken

Within Erin, that pit feeling kept coming up. She knew, deep down, that he wasn't the guy that God intended for her. This was so hard to accept because they were an obvious match in so many ways. They were best friends and so comfortable with each other. Their relationship

> *Erin had to trust God and not settle for someone because he had so many great qualities, when she knew that he wasn't the one for her.*

made so much sense, and neither one wanted it to end. But after three years, they decided to break up. It wasn't easy, and they were both devastated. Their families were just as upset as they were. Their friends were blown away and questioned their decision. In the end, though, Erin had to trust God and not settle for someone because he had so many great qualities, when she knew that he wasn't the one for her or she for him.

Process

Over the past four years since they broke up, Erin has dated a couple of guys but has remained single. She is not looking to date to fill up her time or just be with someone because she doesn't want to be alone. If she goes on a date and finds out that the guy doesn't have the characteristics she is looking for in a husband, such as: he is not a Christian, does drugs, doesn't want to have kids, or there is no emotional connection, she cuts it off right away. She is looking for a relationship, but more importantly, for her husband.

Erin says, "I am human and have desires just like any other young woman. There are days when I do feel lonely and begin to doubt my future or have pity parties. Sometimes I isolate myself and don't want to be around people, but I find that when I focus on others, serve, and get out of my own head, the better off I am.

> *Trust in God: His promises and His timing.*

I've also learned that when I do open up and share how I'm feeling, it opens the door for conversations where I realize that I'm not the only one going through things. The more transparent we are, the more we understand that just about everyone has gone through a 'waiting' season/situation of one kind or another, and we can learn from and encourage each other."

Erin continues: "As cliché as it sounds, I can't do anything but trust in God: His promises and His timing. This is only a *season*; therefore, my aim is to be content with the season I am in because I know it's only temporary. There is a reason that I'm still single, so rather than dwelling on what I don't have right now or what may be missing from my life, I'm taking advantage of the opportunity afforded by my singleness and embracing what I do have and where I am now. I can do certain things to prepare for marriage, but in the meantime, there is plenty else to be done. Sometimes I think I can do so much now because I *am* single. I'm at a time in my life where I can pour myself into my job, my friends, and family, as well as the outreach ministry that I lead at my church (REACH) because I have the time. I know when I'm married and have kids, I won't be able to do all of this, or at least to the extent that I do now because my focus and priorities will shift. My time of being single has allowed me to grow and do things that I might not have otherwise been able to do had I been married."

Hopeful

When the going gets tough, Erin reminds herself that God's ways are not her ways, and His timing is not her timing. She knows that God designed her and knows her better and loves her more than anyone, and she trusts that He designed a great man just for her, who will pursue her and love her like God does. Erin concludes: "God wants the best for me, so my hope is in Him. As time goes on, I continue to learn more and more about who I am and what I want in a relationship and a husband. I don't want to settle for anything/anyone that God doesn't have for me. I've prayed regarding my desire to be married, and it only gets stronger, so I am confident that this is a desire that God has placed in my heart. I may not be sure of when or how things will turn out, but when I let God order my steps, that's the best place I can be. God knows the desires of our hearts! Talk to him and be honest with Him; that's what a relationship is all about. He accepts us and loves us for who we are and is able to do exceedingly abundantly above all that we ask, think, or imagine!"

Key Scriptures God Used to Transform Erin

1. Matthew 16:24 (KJV): If anyone would come after me, let him deny himself and take up his cross and follow me. ^{25} For whoever would save his life will lose it, but whoever

loses his life for my sake will find it. For what will it profit a man if he gains the whole world and forfeits his soul?

2. Galatians 1:10: (NIV): Am I now trying to win the approval of human beings, or of God? Or am I trying to please people? If I were still trying to please people, I would not be a servant of Christ.

3. Matthew 5:13–16 (NIV): You are the salt of the earth. But if the salt loses its saltiness, how can it be made salty again? It is no longer good for anything, except to be thrown out and trampled underfoot. 14 "You are the light of the world. A town built on a hill cannot be hidden. 15 Neither do people light a lamp and put it under a bowl. Instead they put it on its stand, and it gives light to everyone in the house. 16 In the same way, let your light shine before others, that they may see your good deeds and glorify your Father in heaven.

4. Colossians 4:6 (NLT): Let your conversation be gracious and attractive so that you will have the right response for everyone.

5. James 5:8–9 (NIV): For my thoughts are not your thoughts, neither are your ways my ways," declares the Lord. As the heavens are higher than the earth, so are my ways higher than your ways and my thoughts than your thoughts.

6. Jeremiah 29:11 (NIV): For I know the plans I have for you," declares the Lord, "plans to prosper you and not to harm you, plans to give you hope and a future.

7. Psalm 37:4 (NKJV): Delight yourself also in the Lord and He shall give you the desires of your heart.

8. Proverbs 16:9 (NLT): We can make our plans, but the Lord determines our steps.

Sonship Principles

Erin's story models the following sonship principles:

1. Sons and daughters of God resist sin; they do not condone sin in themselves or others. They have the values, priorities, preferences, and tastes of their Father. They are chips off the old block!

2. Sons and daughters of God eat strong meat. This means that we should stop being babies but rather should grow up and train ourselves to distinguish between right and wrong.

3. Sonship is a choice. You and I have a choice in every situation we face to act as a son or as a child. Sonship takes faith and requires obedience to the Holy Spirit. A good indicator of whether or not you are a "son" is in your mind: how you think and what voice you follow. If you are ruled by your emotions, you are a child. If you know what is right to do, but choose to act based on how you feel, you are a child.

4. We are not called to fit in. We are called to rule the planet! God has imbued us with this dual anointing (king and priest) for the express purpose of empowering us to reign on the earth. With this in mind, isn't it amazingly flawed and limiting how much stock we put on trying to fit in and how much resources we expend in trying to accomplish that objective?

5. Sons and daughters of God refuse to settle for a life that is beneath their inheritance, no matter how long and tedious the struggle. This principle is based on the premise that you

cannot change what you tolerate. It is a principle that requires strong personal discipline and a great view of God. Sons and daughters of God believe that God is who He says that He is, and that He would do exactly what He says that He would do. So, they don't negotiate, compromise or settle with the devil, their flesh, or their circumstances. They stand resolute on the word of God, even if they stand alone. They refuse to make room for, accommodate or cohabit with sickness, sin, failure, bondage, defeat and anything else that is beneath who they are in Christ.

6. Not only do "sons" of God refuse to settle for sin and compromise, they also do not settle for the status quo or the convenient. They want everything that God has provided and made available for them. Simply stated, they want their inheritance in God and they are willing to fight for it.

As we grow and mature from children to "sons", we begin to take on the character and characteristics of our heavenly Father. Erin came to know Christ as her Savior when she was nineteen years old, but it took many years after she was saved to submit her mind and life to Him and allow God to transform her from a child into sonship. God desires that we put Him first in everything that we do and say. There will be times when we can live out our beliefs and make an impact without words, but there are other times when we have to take a stand for Christ and speak up. We can't live for the approval and acceptance of people. As we grow into sonship, our desire to put and keep God first, will also grow!

Emotional Healing From Sexual Abuse and Divorce
The Story of Althea Lanier (Alani)

Alani is a beautiful woman, author, mother, business woman, entrepreneur, and minister. She has a BA degree in psychology and a master's degree in human resources. She worked in the human resources field for fifteen years and served as a human resources director for a small nonprofit organization. In 2007, she and her husband decided to become full time entrepreneurs. They bought into a commercial franchise, providing janitorial services. Today, Alani owns, operates, and manages that janitorial business, which has eighteen contracts and twenty employees.

Meet Alani

Emotional Trauma

To the onlooker, Alani's life appears perfect, but it is not. People in her life, male family members, made tragic choices that heaped untold anguish, pain, and heart ache on Alani. The first was when she was a little girl. She was taken advantage of and sexually

190

abused by her dad for a very long time. From the last episode of this abuse, it took her over twenty years to summon up enough courage to say the word *incest* or the softer phase *family sexual abuse* out loud and not feel something negative and derogatory about herself. It has been a long journey to healing from this dirty little family secret. Alani's book, *A Family Secret Revealed: More Than a Story* chronicles her journey of survival.

The second bout of emotional anguish came in October 2012. Alani had survived long-term childhood sexual abuse, and had grown into a beautiful and productive young woman. At the age of twenty-six, after three years of dating and one year of engagement, she married her "supportive" best friend. They created and shared a wonderful life together. It was picture perfect to everyone who knew them. She did everything she knew to be a wonderful wife. She loved her husband and treated him like a king. She was committed to her children and was an awesome and loving mom. She and her husband worked as close friends and partners in raising their two beautiful and amazing daughters.

All that changed in October 2012. On October 31, just three months after their eighteenth wedding anniversary, the life she knew changed drastically overnight. On that day, this wonderful man and love of her life stabbed her in the heart with a double edged sword. He came home that night and she heard words from him that she never expected to hear. "I've been lying to you for a long time. I've not been happy; I've had an affair, and I'm leaving!"

So, just like that, after twenty two years of courtship and marriage, Alani experienced an unexpected separation and eventual divorce. It took her a while to regain her composure, overcome her initial shock, and decide how to manage her newfound single status. The following year, she decided to study for her commercial driver's license. She became a fixed route bus operator for Delaware Transit Corporation. She drove buses on a part-time basis for a year and then full time for another year. She received a promotion to a supervisor and then another promotion to a compliance specialist in the office of civil rights. Alani not only survived; she thrived!

Healing

During this time, God was doing an amazing work of healing and restoration in Alani! God not only healed her, but He began to use her as a minister of His grace to restore wholeness to lives that are devastated by emotional hurt. Out of the crucible of her pain and tears emerged a new life giving ministry. Alani, which stands for "Advocating Liberation and Non-Oppression in Individuals" became a lifeline of hope and restoration for so many. Alani began in 2010 as a ministry focused on emotional healing from family sexual abuse, but in 2012, it was redefined and expanded to include all types of emotional hurt and trauma. Today, Alani facilitates emotional healing small groups through the BRIDGE Technique. BRIDGE stands for "Breaking ground, root defining, interceding, discovering, growing, and executing." This Bridge technique is designed to help people to go from a place of tragedy to triumph after experiencing hurt.

Alani says: "As I think about these two emotionally painful life experiences, I think about a quote from *Virginia Satir:* "Life is not the way it's supposed to be. It's the way it is. The way you cope with it is what makes the difference." I was not supposed to have been sexually abused by my dad. I was not supposed to have been dropped like a hot potato, forcing me into divorce after being the wife most men would dream of having. These are two of the most difficult and tragic experiences of my life. Both my dad and my former husband made choices that negatively impacted my world causing me to reap emotional pain."

But Alani is not a quitter! She is strong, bold, and very courageous. She has unwavering faith in God and boldly declares His Word. Alani believes in herself! She affirms her confidence in herself and her God with daily affirmations.

Alani's Affirmations

Alani has some affirmations that help her to stand strong and maintain a perspective of victory and triumph through life's circumstances. Here they are:

This is me from A to Z

This is me from A to Z.
I am amazing and bodacious.
1 am confident and desirable.
I am eloquent and funny.
I am God's beloved.
I am happy and intelligent.
I am joy-filled & knowledgeable.
I am love.
I am a masterpiece and a phenomenal woman. I am queen B (as in beautiful, inside and out).
I am resilient and spiritual.
I am a treasure and unique.
I am a virtuous woman.
I am wise and x-traordinary.

I am youthful and I am zealous. Yes—this is me from A to Z!!!!!

> Nonsense has an expiration date!

The Freedom Igniter Affirmation

I awake every morning with a smile on my face and happiness, contentment, and gratitude in my heart! Why? Because nonsense has an expiration date *and* I have learned to accept what God allows!

Key Scriptures God Used to Heal Alani

1. Psalm 37:23 (NKJV): The steps of a good man/ woman are ordered by the Lord and he delights in his way. Though he falls, he shall not be utterly cast down, for the Lord upholds him with his hand.

2. Philippians 4:8 (AMP): Finally, believers, whatever is true, whatever is honorable *and* worthy of respect, whatever is right *and* confirmed by God's word, whatever is pure *and* wholesome, whatever is lovely *and* brings peace, whatever is admirable *and* of good repute; if there is any excellence, if there is anything worthy of praise, think continually on these things center your mind on them, and implant them in your heart.

3. Philippians 4:13 (AMP): I can do all things through Him who strengthens *and* empowers me to fulfill His purpose. I am self-sufficient in Christ's sufficiency; I am ready for anything

and equal to anything through Him who infuses me with inner strength and confident peace.

4. Isaiah 54:17 (AMP) "No weapon that is formed against you will succeed; And every tongue that rises against you in judgment you will condemn.

Sonship Principles

Alani's story models the following sonship principles:

1. I must recognize my personal value and own it.

2. Self-talk is very important because it outlines the image of myself I have on the inside. My self-image is critical because what I believe and say about myself has the greatest impact on my life more than any other person's words spoken over me. As a son or daughter of God, I must be able to say to myself with deep conviction, "I have something of great value to offer others—myself and who I am in Christ."

3. Simply stated, the Word of God coming out of my mouth, in faith, is the most potent weapon known to man. What this means is that every word I speak is on assignment. Once I believe the word in my heart and launch it forth via the spoken word, it will not return empty; it will achieve its creative purpose and assignment. It is unstoppable!

4. I win in life, only when I recognize and embrace my personal value in Christ. Winners say, *I can*. That confidence comes from a deeper I AM. For a believer, that confidence comes from knowing who I am and whose I am. I belong to God. I am a son or daughter of Almighty God I am seated in heavenly places in Christ Jesus. All things are possible to

me because I believe. Sons and daughters of God say "*I am so I can.*"

> *Winners say "I can". That confidence comes from a deeper, "I AM."*

Alani's affirmations come from a deep knowledge of who she is in Christ. It is a recognition that her self-worth and identity is not tied to the rejection and abuse she experienced at the hands of her dad and former husband. Her "*I am*" affirmations are empowering self-talk that have helped her walk a path to freedom from trauma and enabled her to blaze that same trail for others.

Triumph

Alani is a firm believer that everything in her life is orchestrated by God. He knew that tragedy would strike in her life, but He also already paved a road to victory called triumph! He knew she was ready and equipped to survive every dart the adversary threw at her. He knew that through these ashes of pain and trauma, the work of ALANI would be forthcoming. She says, "Since God cared that much for me and had that much faith in me, I have no other choice but to be faithful to Him; I am compelled to be obedient in whatever task He assigns to my hands."

When all is said and done, Alani's desire is to help those who have been overcome by emotional hurt and pain to realize that in spite of that, they can live a fruitful and productive life! To learn more about this ministry, please visit www.alani.org or Alani, The Freedom Igniter on Facebook.

From Janitor to Corporate Officer
The Story of Kenneth J. Parker

He was a senior executive and consummate professional with over thirty years outstanding experience in the energy industry. He worked with executive, legislative, and regulatory officials at the national, state, and local levels as well as community leaders, business leaders, and nonprofits in New Jersey, Delaware, Maryland, and the District of Columbia. He is recognized for his exceptional ability to successfully design and implement strategies for stakeholder engagement and issues management. He has held a key role in three successful energy utility mergers. His leadership strengths include networking and building collaborative strategic relationships. He is Kenneth J. Parker, former senior vice president of governmental and external affairs for Pepco Holdings, Inc. an Exelon Company. Ken was accountable within the government affairs space and excellent at what he did. He served on the executive committee of Pepco Holdings, Inc. and reported to the chairman and CEO. Like the other executives in the room, Ken looked like he belonged there, and he did! However, his path to success, is unlike any other executive in the room. By all accounts, he should have been a statistic, but rather, he was a top executive in a Fortune 500 company. His story is probably one of the most inspirational stories you would ever hear. It is a story of faith, love, courage, hard work and perseverance, as well as family and community support.

Ken joined Atlantic City Electric in 1986 as a summer intern helper in the landscaping department. He cut the lawn and maintained the grounds. Later that year, he became the service building attendant, a position he held until 1990, when he was promoted to Distribution

Right-of-Way Representative. Ken progressed through a series of promotions with increasing responsibility; from senior government legislative representative/analyst in 1994; to manager, customer and community relations, regional account manager; manager of government affairs; assistant vice president, regional vice president, and ultimately, regional president of Atlantic City Electric Company. Altogether, Ken held over fifteen jobs with the company and retired in 2017 as the senior vice president of governmental and external affairs, reporting to the CEO of Pepco Holdings, an Exelon company.

Humble Beginnings

Ken was born and raised in southern New Jersey with five sisters and four brothers. He was the ninth of ten children. His mother, Ella Melba Parker, died of heart complications when he was two years old. She was only forty one years old. His father, Willie Lee Parker, distraught over the loss of his wife and overwhelmed by the prospect of raising ten children, ran off to Florida, leaving Ken and his siblings in Winslow Township located in Camden County, New Jersey, to fend for themselves. Shortly thereafter, while still in Florida, Ken's father was shot and killed. So, by the tender age of two years old, Ken was an orphan. The deaths of both his parents changed Ken's life dramatically, placing him and several of his siblings in the New Jersey Foster Care System for seven years.

This is where the amazing first turn for good in this tragic story happens. Ken's eldest sister, Patricia, twenty years his senior, made a personal sacrifice to take care of her siblings. She was only twenty two years old at the time of these tragic family circumstances, but she rose to the occasion. Patricia was a young woman herself, a recent graduate from Glassboro Teacher's College (now Rowan

University), and a teacher in a neighboring community. Ken explains, "My sister Patricia was a guardian angel who never left me and my siblings. After our parents died, she was focused on taking care of us."

Due to circumstances, several siblings were moved into foster care, but she stayed close to us. She tried her best to ensure that we were placed with good families and remained in constant contact with us. She would work with the foster parents to take us home for the weekend and to tutor us. I never felt alone; I always knew that she would come to visit."

Patricia Parker

Eventually, when Ken was twelve years old, Patricia was able to get her siblings out of the foster care system and back together under one roof. She took on the role of guardian and became the parental figure of the family, caring for her siblings until they could move on to college or whatever path they chose. The close knit bond initiated by Patricia is the tie that continues to hold Ken and his siblings together. Even up to this day, Patricia is the matriarch of the Parker family. She is always there when Ken and family members need support and advice.

Growing Up

Ken was educated in the Winslow Township Elementary Schools and at Edgewood Middle and High Schools located in Southern New Jersey, living in various sections of Winslow, Blue Anchor and Sicklerville, New Jersey. Ken remembers his childhood as one of fun and adventure, especially in the summer. Whether it was fishing, camping, playing on local sports teams, or participating in the summer basketball competition, Ken remembers a time of peace and love. He says, "I have always felt God's presence in my life. I felt protected. I felt He sent special people from all walks of life to help me grow and develop." Patricia, Ken's sister, states that "Ken was a happy-go-lucky young man who loved to play outdoors. He also loved to entertain the family with his singing and dancing."

> *I have always felt God's presence in my life. I felt protected.*

Being the ninth of ten children, high expectations were set for Ken by the family, school, and community. Pursuing high school graduation requirements and attending college was a clear expectation. Under the direction of Patricia, Ken's family decided that the best way to honor the memory of their parents was to meet the goals that had been set for them by their parents. So, they pulled together to help one another succeed. Ken was an average student but had great interpersonal skills and could get along quickly with anybody. Academics was always stressed by his family, and he loved the school's extracurricular activities. He loved to play basketball, but his freedom to play was contingent on successful completion of his school work and other academic programs.

> *My sister Patricia was a guardian angel who never left me and my siblings.*

Ken the Janitor

Ken attended Delaware State University, Dover, and in 1990, earned a bachelor of science degree in early childhood education. It took him approximately nine years, post high school, to reach this goal. Ken said, "I decided not to go back to college in my senior year to finish my degree because there was a permanent job I wanted to obtain within the company." That job, was the service building attendant. Ken was the only applicant and was offered the union job. In that capacity, he worked the overnight shift. He was responsible for cleaning the buildings and dispatching utility crews to address customer concerns. Eventually Ken went back to college and completed his degree.

He was well acquainted with work, as he began working at the age of fourteen. His motto was: "I'll do all the work to the best of my ability as long as it's legal." Pride in self and work was a daily theme in the Parker home. They were taught to do their current job to the best of their ability, as if it was their last job.

Reflecting on his work ethic, Ken says: "You have to do every job well. I do not let the job demean me. When I worked as a landscaper, I never thought, "I'm just a landscaper." When I worked as a service buildings attendant, I cleaned the floors until they were spotless. People knew who worked that shift. They wrote notes to say, 'You've done an outstanding job.' I strived to master every job because my work is a reflection of me. You can't just do your job halfway. I felt blessed to have a job."

Ken the Family Man

Ken met his wife Sheri when he was a service building attendant. Sheri, a former public school teacher, is a woman of quiet poise and dignity. They were married in 1990, long before he became a corporate success story. Ken gives honor and praise to Sheri, his wife of twenty eight years, who has loved, encouraged and supported him unconditionally. She is his rock, and without her, he feels that he would have lost his way! Ken says: "She didn't marry me for how much money I made. She married me for the person I am, and that's the greatest thing. That's true love. She has always been a true champion of mine and a supporter. The stability that she provided helped me develop as a young man."

Ken and family. From left to right, Ken Jr, Lauren, Sheri and Ken Sr.

Ken and Sheri have two wonderful young adult children: Ken Jr. and Lauren. Coming from a legacy of abandonment by his dad, Ken was determined early on to make a lifelong commitment to his family. He purposed in his heart to stay in the partnership with his wife and children for life. To learn how to be a good father, he would watch

TV for positive role models of what a father should be and apply the lessons he learned. He also had role models from the community. Learning and applying these lessons helped him to become a better husband and father. Also, Sheri's dad, his father-in-law, was a tremendous coach, mentor, and role model; teaching and coaching Ken on how to be a godly man, husband, and father. Ken says, "I plan to hang in there and be supportive of my wife and children until I transition from this earth. I have a great example in my sister Pat. She never left us."

Ken's In laws, George and Anita McLaurin

Ken the Public Official

It is nothing short of amazing how Ken, a major in early childhood education, would excel in a high profile job working with politicians and elected officials. Asked about that, Ken told the story of his other sister, Aletha. Aletha, who has since passed away, was a well-respected public official in Camden City, New Jersey. She worked tirelessly to help the poor, homeless, and people in need of support.

Ken explains, "I was criticizing the local school board and saying that they need to do better. My sister Aletha said, "You can sit back and criticize. It's not as easy as you think. Maybe you should run for the school board to see what it means to be in that leadership position and to make a difference." So, at twenty three years of age, Ken ran for election to the Winslow Township Board of Education. Even though he lost, he learned how to mobilize the grassroots, put together a platform and solicit votes.

Ken recalls that experience, "I lost my first election. Being young and naive, I thought I could just change the world. I learned you have to have support. I learned about policy and politics from other members who were fifteen or twenty years older than me. I lost my first election by a wide margin, but in the next election, I was the highest vote getter. I learned to knock on doors to earn votes. Later, I got involved in my sister Aletha's elections." Ken served as a school board member for six years. He used what he learned about interpersonal relationships while on the school board to help him navigate his way through his career and in Washington, DC.

During college and while working at Atlantic City Electric, Ken always made time to help his community and give back to his hometown, Winslow Township, New Jersey. In addition to mentoring high school and college kids, he is very passionate about young people in the foster care system. Both his sister Patricia and his wife Sheri firmly suggested that he broaden his outreach beyond foster care because there are a lot of kids out there who need help. Ken says, "It is important that we help young people realize their lives can be much more than what they perceive it to be. We must show up to share our experiences and help them."

It Takes a Village

Throughout his life, Ken faced many challenges and obstacles. He and his siblings saw their family face issues of unemployment, drugs, alcohol, mental illness, physical disabilities, learning disabilities, physical abuse, incarceration, homelessness, and various other challenges. Despite these challenges, Ken remembers the opportunities that were offered to him and the ones that he chose to accept to improve his own life. He understands how faith, perseverance, family, education, hard work, community support, and caring people have influenced his life. Ken recognizes and values the contribution others have made to his success. He explains: "There has always been somebody, an angel, divine intervention, or just a kind passerby who showed up and helped me every step of the way. They have come from all walks of life and different ethnicities. It is literally a rainbow of people who have helped me succeed."

Ken does not remember his mom and dad. He only knows what he has been told by family and friends. His mother loved her children and cleaned homes, and his father was a hard worker on farms in South Jersey. His mother left a strong legacy for Ken and his siblings, a legacy of helping others. A plaque hangs in Ken's home, with their mother's favorite saying: "Don't down the one who is down today. Help them in their sorrow. This ol' world is a funny ol' world. You may be down tomorrow." That saying is a beacon that has guided Ken's life. Ken says: "I love my mom and dad unconditionally. I don't understand why my dad left our family, and I will not make excuses for him. I am a person of faith, and I believe that one day I will have the opportunity to reunite with my parents again."

Ken's journey has taught him that everyone has a story to tell about challenges, learning from mistakes, failures, overcoming obstacles, and seizing opportunities. Ken is a lifelong learner. He learned a lot from his family. From his sister Patricia, he learned to be honest, truthful, support his family, and stay committed. From his sister Aletha, he learned the art and finesse of interpersonal relationships and the importance of helping others. He is a strong believer in helping and encouraging others to persevere and achieve their goals. He believes that one way to do this is by telling your personal story to help inspire others to keep the faith.

When asked "Did you think you would get this far?" Ken's answer was emphatic "No, I never thought I would get this far. It all goes back to the fundamentals of what I've been taught: just do the job that you have well, and things will work themselves out. That's what I try to communicate to the younger people as well." Ken credits his success to God, determination, hard work, family, his fraternity, and community support. There were many people, both in the community and school, who provided a little extra guidance and saw the possibilities in him. This has been true throughout his entire life. Ken strongly believes that you must have faith in yourself, help others and never give up!

Key Scripture God Used to Empower Ken

Job 8:7 states, "Though thy beginning was small, yet thy latter end should greatly increase."

Sonship Principles

Ken's story models the following sonship principles:

1. God has placed tremendous value in us, all of us— He calls us sons and daughters! We are sons and daughters of God. We are heirs of God and joint heirs with Christ. We have the DNA of God. We

> *God is my source of origin, and that source will never diminish in value. So, nothing and no one can truly devalue me.*

are partakers of His divine nature. We are of inestimable value. The value of a thing is measured by how much people are willing to pay for it. Jesus gave His life for us, and that defines our value as sons and daughters of God.

2. My value comes from my source. It does not come from my performance, whether or not people like me, how much money I have, my net worth, who I know, what I drive, how I look, and so on. God is my source of origin, and that source will never diminish in value. So, nothing and no one can truly devalue me. In his book, *25 Ways to Win with People*, John Maxwell provided a vivid illustration. A $100 bill may be crumpled, tossed on the ground, stepped on, and ground into the dust, but it will never lose its value. It is still a $100 bill and legal tender for goods and services regardless of how dirty or crumpled it is. The same analogy is applicable to us as human beings. We may be dropped, crumpled, ground into the dust, and dirtied by life, but that will never devalue us because our value comes from God, our Creator, not from our status, circumstances, or other people.

3. Owning my personal value allows me to be authentic. God wants me to be authentic. He made me an original. I must be comfortable in my own skin. I am an uncommon package, with my issues, challenges, personality, quirks, skin color, ethnicity, and so forth. I was uniquely put together by God and assigned a unique identifier—my fingerprint. I am one of a kind. Nothing about me is an accident. Authenticity is God's permission to be what He designed me to be.

4. The scripture is clear! Before I was born, before I had a chance to do good or bad, God loved me, chose me in Christ, and decided to adopt me into His family. So, I do not deserve or merit God's blessings or goodness based on my

works, ability, performance, prayer, fasting, obedience, or service. Faith in the finished works of Christ on the cross is my only access and claim to God's forgiveness for my sins and everything else that God has.

Ken's childhood and life story along with his career path from landscaper to corporate officer within a Fortune 500 company are both extraordinary and inspirational. When asked what qualities contributed to his success, Ken lists perseverance, interpersonal skills, getting along with people, building strong and supportive networks, and a good work ethic. Now that he is retired, he enjoys spending time with his immediate family and mentoring his nephews, nieces, and others. Watching them succeed and achieve their goals gives him great joy. Ken sums up the story of his life quite nicely "To God be the glory!"

Proclamation

I am a son/daughter of God. I am an heir of God and a joint heir with Christ. I say, thank you Lord, for all that you have done for me! Great are you Lord, and greatly to be praised. My father, you reign in power and great glory. You reign as King of Kings and Lord of Lords. I praise and exalt your glorious name, King of the universe. I acknowledge that every good and perfect gift comes from you. And I thank you for your abundant goodness. Now unto You, the King eternal, immortal, invisible, the only wise God, be honor and glory forever and ever! Amen.

To God be the glory!

CONCLUSION

My vision in writing this book is to empower every Christian to fulfill their sonship mandate and walk in victory as a son or daughter of God. Sonship is our birthright and God our Father wants us to occupy and rule over the earth, acting in His stead, as God. This book provides a clear understanding of what it means to be a "son" of God, clarifies that new covenant sonship is gender neutral, empowers you, the reader, to walk in the rights and privileges of sonship, challenges you to replicate the sonship pattern modeled by Christ, and enables you to transition from childhood into sonship. It concludes with stories of people whose lives have been transformed by the principles in this book.

Choosing to walk as a mature son or daughter of God is not a "once-and-done" enterprise. It is a daily choice to say yes to God and no to your flesh, the world, sin, and the devil. It is an immensely rewarding walk of discipline, obedience, faith and victory. God Himself is your reward as His presence floods your being and His image is emblazoned on your heart and manifest in your daily walk and talk.

To help you in the sonship quest, we have presented stories of men and women who made a choice, often in horrific circumstances, to apply the sonship principles in the Bible and walk the sonship trail blazed by Christ Himself. I pray that their determination, perseverance, commitment, obedience, courage, and subsequent victory will encourage and challenge you to win in whatever circumstances you find yourself.

My earnest prayer is that you will fulfill your sonship mandate and walk as a "son" of God in the earth—Amen!

ACKNOWLEDGMENTS

1. Every book is the result of the work of a team, and this book is no exception.

2. Thank you to my friend and partner the Holy Spirit, at whose persistent nudging I finally wrote this book.

3. Thanks to my children, Emmanuel, Timothy and Rhema, whose support, encouragement and love kept me motivated.

4. Thanks to the Sons of God Program team - Kwame Sakah, Felicia Owusu, Luke and Vivalyn Elvy, Emmanuel Asamoah and Rhema Godson – whose partnership made the weekly Sons of God Program successful.

5. Thanks to my family and friends who reviewed the manuscript.

6. Thanks to the men and women whose stories are in chapter 5, who through their lives illustrate the power and principles of sonship.

7. Thanks to my project team at Xulon Press, Sylvia Burleigh, Greg Dixon, Callan Fitzgerald and the whole team.

8. I am deeply grateful to God my Father, for His grace that has kept me and for the privilege of writing this book.

9. This book is a joint effort by many. I am truly grateful for the opportunity to partner with you all. I am better because of you.

ENDNOTES

CHAPTER 1: THE NEW DEAL

1. Billy Graham, "The Power of the Cross", Decision Magazine, January 23, 2007.

2. Rick Renner, "The Cross! Foolishness or the Power of God", Sparkling Gems Volume 11, October 17, 2017.

CHAPTER 2: A PORTRAIT OF NEW COVENANT SONSHIP

1. John Piper, "The Spirit-Led Are the Sons of God", Desiring God, April 14, 2002.

2. Bob Sullivan, "Identity Theft is Skyrocketing, and Getting More Sophisticated", MarketWatch, February 27, 2018.

CHAPTER 3: SEVEN POWERFUL PRINCIPLES ON HOW TO WALK IN VICTORY AS A SON OF GOD

1. John Maxwell, 25 Ways to Win with People, Thomas Nelson, 2005.

2. Dr. Charles Stanley, "Making Decisions God's Way", Daily Devotional, February 05, 2015.

3. Dr. Charles Stanley, "A Defense Against Temptation", Daily Devotional, December 17, 2017.

4. "How Did Jesus Learn Obedience and Become Perfect?" Interview with John Piper, Founder and Teacher, DesiringGod.org, June 30, 2016.

5. Ibid

6. Charles Dickens, Oliver Twist, Dodd, Mead & Co., 1941.

CHAPTER 4: JESUS, GOD'S SONSHIP PATTERN

1. Daniel Graves, *Article #2,* "You are the Christ, the Son of the Living God"
2. Ibid

CHAPTER 5: MANIFESTATIONS

1. Kenneth & Gloria Copeland, Healing Promises, Kenneth Copeland Publications, 1994.
2. Elisabeth Kubler-Ross, "On Death and Dying", Simon & Schuster/Touchstone, 1969.
3. Vivalyn A. Elvy, "Who Am I?", Redemption Press, 2017.
4. Dennis Sellers, "Rick Warren Quotes on Faith: 7 Memorable Statements From Christian Evangelist", May 28, 2015.
5. ALANI, "A Family Secret Revealed: More Than a Story", Legacy Book Publishing, 2012.
6. Virginia Satir Quotes. "BrainyQuote.com", BrainyMedia Inc, 2018

OTHER BOOKS BY THE AUTHOR

Reclaim Your Destiny, 31 Day Proclamations to Build Christ Esteem And Godly Self Image, *LifeWork Press, 2022*

The Colt Story, LifeWork Press, 2021

I AM The God Kind, Living in the Reality of Your Identity in Christ, LifeWork Press, 2021

Fight to Win with Prayer and Proclamations, LifeWork Press 2020.

Choosing a Life of Victory, Xulon Press 2019.

Single and Happy, Are You A W.H.O.L.E Single? Xulon Press 2019.

Single and Happy, Are You A W.H.O.L.E Single? Study Guide.

Workbook: 5 Practical Steps to Wholeness in Spirit, Soul, and Body.

AUTHOR MINISTRY RESOURCES

LIFEWORK MINISTRIES, INC.
LifeWork Ministries empowers people to live the abundant life in Christ. We preach, write, and witness! Our compelling mission is to release the Life of Christ into the world by using our faith, thinking our faith, speaking our faith, singing our faith, praying our faith and sharing our faith. Connect with us on our website: **www.lifeworkministries.org** or send us an email at **lifeworkministriesinc@gmail.com**

WEEKLY RADIO BROADCAST
Gloria has a weekly Bible teaching program on REACH Gospel Radio and the Wilkins Radio network. You can hear her radio broadcast in cities across America. For the schedule of her weekly radio bible teaching program, please go to our website: **www.lifeworkministries.org.**

LICENSED CLINICAL PASTORAL COUNSELOR & TEMPERAMENT COUNSELOR
At LifeWork Ministries, we provide individual, family, marriage, pre-marital, relationship, career, ministry, and teen counseling. Contact us on our website at **www.lifeworkministries.org**

iDECLARE PRAYER AND PROCLAMATION
Gloria hosts the iDECLARE Prayer and Proclamation event. The word of God, spoken in faith, is the most powerful weapon known to man. At iDECLARE, we load, cock, and fire the word of God to transform our lives, families, and nations!

RACIAL EQUITY & UNITY

Gloria leads the Biblical Equity and Unity (BEU) collaborative, hosts the monthly BEU Community dialogue and the annual Racial Equity and Unity luncheon. Our vision is to educate, engage, and advocate on issues of biblical equity and unity; and to promote racial reconciliation and healing. Facebook@REUofDE.

SAVED SINGLES SUMMIT

Gloria hosts the Saved Singles Summit, a premier Christ-centered forum, which brings together Christian singles from churches across America for a time of fun, fellowship, empowerment, kingdom connections and new opportunities. Join us at: **www.savedsinglessummit.com**. Facebook@savedsinglessummit.

SINGLE CHRISTIANS CONNECT MEETUP GROUPS

For clean, fun, weekly activities and social events.
**https://www.meetup.com/single-christians-connect/
https://www.meetup.com/philadelphia_single_Christians-connect/**

SINGLE SENSE CONVERSATIONS

Monthly fun, interactive, Zoom panel discussion on singles issues, every 4th Friday.

THE GRACETALK

Weekly internet talk show hosted by Gloria on Sundays at 6pm:
https://www.facebook.com/TheGraceTalk/live_videos/

ABOUT THE AUTHOR

Gloria Godson is a multi-faceted corporate executive, with an illustrious career in the Energy Industry. She is a visionary, thought and strategy leader, and consummate senior executive. An attorney by training, she rose through several executive leadership positions to become a Vice President in Exelon Corporation, the largest energy company in America.

Most importantly, Gloria is a Christian leader, Bible teacher, author, prayer minister, and conference speaker. She is a Licensed Clinical Pastoral Counselor, Certified Temperament Counselor and Professional Clinical Member of the National Christian Counselors Association. She is the CEO of LifeWork Ministries, and has a weekly Bible teaching radio program. She hosts Wholeness Workshops, Temperament Workshops, the premier annual Saved Singles Summit, the iDECLARE Prayer and Proclamation event, the Racial Equity and Unity Community Events, and the live *GraceTalk* internet talk show.

Gloria served on the Board of Word of Life (WOL) Christian Center in Newark, Delaware, a full gospel, non-denominational church, for over twelve years. And for over fifteen years, Gloria also served as overseer of the WOL prayer ministries, and is a regular eye witness to God's miraculous answers to prayer. She is a powerful minister of the word of God, with a singular focus on building lives and the kingdom of God. She is a dynamic speaker who connects with both professional and Christian audiences across the country and around the world.

Gloria loves to serve her community! She is on the Board of Faith and Freedom Coalition Mid-Atlantic. Gloria is an online missionary with Global Media Outreach, a dedicated volunteer with the REACH community outreach, the Sunday Breakfast Mission, Urban Promise, Exceptional Care for Children, and more. She loves God passionately and believes in the unstoppable power of Almighty God to do the impossible. She has three children and lives in Delaware, United States.

AUTHOR CONTACT

To invite Gloria to speak, send her your prayer request, place a book order, or simply connect, please go to:

www.lifeworkministries.org

www.gloriagodson.com

Facebook@TheGraceTalk

Instagram@TheGraceTalk

YouTube@TheGraceTalk

LifeWork Ministries, Inc.

P. O. Box 56,

Townsend, DE 19734

www.lifeworkministries.org

EMAIL

lifeworkministriesinc@gmail.com

www.ingramcontent.com/pod-product-compliance
Lightning Source LLC
LaVergne TN
LVHW040140080526
838202LV00042B/2962